Jobfinder

Christine Ingham

FOURTH ESTATE • London

First published in Great Britain in 1997 by
Fourth Estate Limited
6 Salem Road
London W2 4BU

1 3 5 7 9 10 8 6 4 2

A catalogue record for this book is available from the British Library.

ISBN 1–85702–630–6

Typeset by York House Typographic Ltd.
Printed in Great Britain by Clays Ltd, St. Ives plc, Bungay, Suffolk

Jobfinder

Christine Ingham is a full-time writer on careers and employment. A former secondary school teacher, she has published several books and previously set up an employment project with the Rathbone Society.

Also by the author

In this series
Interviews

Life Without Work
Working Well at Home
New Work Options
101 Ways to Start Your Own Business

Contents

specifications – Fringe benefits – Filling out the picture – Do I proceed?

Acknowledgements

I gratefully acknowledge the assistance of the people and organisations without whose help this book would be less than complete, including CEEFAX, the Department for Education and Employment, the Federation of Recruitment and Employment Services, the Halifax Building Society, the Higher Education Careers Services Unit, ICI, the Institute of Personnel and Development, Intertexec, Manpower Employment Services, Marks and Spencer, the National Council for Vocational Qualifications, Teletext and the University of London.

C.I., March 1997

An Introduction to Jobfinding

THE NEW CERTAINTY

Benjamin Franklin once said that nothing is certain in life except death and taxes. Writing in 1789, little did he realise that two hundred years later, as the second millennium comes to a close, another certainty would creep into life: paradoxically it is the state of *un*certainty.

This mobile new world has emerged out of rapid changes with which employers have had to wrestle and to which they have had to respond: new global markets; worldwide competition; new technologies, demanding new skills; moves away from manufacturing to service industries; upturns and downturns in economies.

As a result of these ongoing changes, employers have had to bring into being new operational and management structures in order not only to survive but to become more competitive – not just with neighbouring businesses as before, but also with companies in other countries. At its most basic, being competitive has meant paring costs to the bone, becoming more responsive to changing markets and economic situations and thereby (hopefully) making more profits. This new focus has meant employers have changed, perhaps for ever, the experience of work for millions of people. To achieve their ends they have introduced the concept of flexibility as the norm and multi-skilling as a must. Delayering and downsizing have left many highly skilled professionals strewn across the wasteland of what was once their working homeland – often on more than one occasion in their careers.

Changes on this scale have made unexpected, sometimes radical, demands on people throughout the workforce, at all levels. The reality of change is upon us. Secure guarantees of continuous, regular employment in a stable work environment appear to be slipping into history.

Faced with this new reality, becoming adept at jobhunting is the new imperative, not just while pinning down the first job after school or graduation, not just while scouting for the second job and not just while an unexpected period of unemployment is vanquished. Jobhunting is a key skill for life. It's worth getting it right. That is the aim of this book.

WHAT EMPLOYERS WANT

To succeed at jobhunting it isn't enough to chase single-mindedly after vacancies without understanding what the market-place is itself demanding. What employers want goes beyond the remit of a job title. Sometimes they inform would-be applicants explicitly what they're looking for via job descriptions, person specifications and selection criteria (Chapter 4), but they don't always. And even if they do, they may not spell out those elements which, when they see them in a candidate, will prove decisive and lead quickly to the offer of the job.

So what do they look for? We can all be forgiven for thinking they only want to see paper qualifications, and indeed it is true that qualifications significantly increase a person's chance of finding work. But that is only part of the story.

It is essential to demonstrate reliability, honesty, openness and other appropriate personal traits related to the workplace. Employers want to see a positive, professional attitude in a well-balanced applicant. They report problems recruiting people with sound *basic* educational skills – even graduates. Successful jobfinders will have equipped themselves well with the fundamentals of reading, writing, oral communication and numeracy.

Surprisingly, employers have also said that technical skills are less important than personal qualities; they reckon that skills can always be taught – a good attitude to work can't.

Employers attach a lot more importance to general skills which can be transferred to any work environment, like:

◆ problem-solving skills

◆ communication skills

◆ the ability to organise and manage your workload

◆ reasoning skills

◆ interpersonal skills.

Having skills in information technology – knowledge of computer programs, keyboarding skills, experience of the Internet – relevant to the type of work sought can also give a boost to an application in the eyes of an employer.

Because of the changes in how businesses are structured and operate, employers are now increasingly looking for those personal competences in employees which they would previously have expected to find only in managers – things like:

◆ leadership

◆ initiative

◆ motivation

◆ decisiveness.

In fact British Telecom cites three which they see becoming increasingly important and which they now look for in all employees: flexibility, adaptability and being able to cope with uncertainty. 'Flexibility' appears to be on every employer's lips. Being able to show commitment to the success of the business is also cited as being important, according to the Institute of Personnel and Development.

In addition, showing general business awareness and an appreciation of those elements which make up the larger picture, such as customer-focused approaches, results orientation and the importance of quality, will warm the heart and soul of any employer.

GIVING EMPLOYERS WHAT THEY WANT

Knowing what employers want, the successful jobfinder must find a way of using the application process to demonstrate that knowledge – in the written application (Chapters 3, 5 and 6) and at interview. The careful filling in of an application form or writing of a covering letter will demonstrate some of the key basic educational skills which employers look for. Referring in an application to situations which indicate traits such as reliability, determination to succeed, or particular personal skills will not go unnoticed. Interviews can be used to reveal your key personal competences. At each stage in the application process it is vital to be aware of what employers are looking for and how you can show them you have what they want.

Unfortunately, they won't accept unsubstantiated assertions of flexibility, keenness and good team-working skills. They expect evidence. Even if you're currently not in paid employment, it will help to increase jobhunting success if you can demonstrate your continuing involvement in your chosen career, along with ongoing experience of the workplace. Setting up your own work-experience programme, doing voluntary work in which you can practise or extend your skills, continuing with work-related learning – all are evidence of commitment.

JOBHUNTING SKILLS

To be able to put personal and professional skills into practice by getting a job, jobhunting skills must first be developed. The rest of the book concentrates on the specifics, but the following are general skills and qualities which also play their part in making jobfinding activities effective:

- ◆ good organisation and preparation

- ◆ persistence

- ◆ good communication (also mentioned by employers)

- ◆ networking skills (see Chapter 2)

- confidence in your own abilities

- research skills

- good interview skills (see Chapter 7)

- enthusiasm

- flexibility of approach – if successive applications fail, be prepared to learn from the experience.

Being able to hang on to the towel instead of throwing it in is also pretty vital. There may be times when every effort seems futile, particularly after a rejection. Developing a philosophical approach to handling the 'No, thank yous' is important.

- Think about what can be learned from failed applications to help the next one move closer to success.

- Remember there are other applications to pursue.

IN THE MEANTIME

Looking for work is far from being the sole preserve of people who are registered unemployed. Career-changers, promotion seekers, contract workers, students, returners to work and returning expats are among the many groups of people looking for new employment at any one time. Although the reasons which prompt a search for work may be quite diverse, all have the same end in sight: a new job.

For those with a full timetable, because of work or other commitments, finding the spare time in which to jobhunt can prove difficult. For unemployed people (registered or not) the reverse is more likely. Scanning advertised vacancies in the newspaper can take minutes, not hours. How can those vast remaining tracts of time possibly be constructively occupied with jobhunting? Chapters 1, 2, 3 and 4 will reveal all.

Unemployed or under-employed jobseekers often encounter another problem: what to say in social situations or at interview when asked what they do for a living. Even though being unemployed has lost much of the social stigma previously attached to it (mainly because we all realise that no one is immune – not even bank managers), it can be uncomfortable to have nothing more than a mumbled 'I'm unemployed' to fall back on. With potential employers especially, try to veer away from defining yourself by what you are not – that is, 'I'm *un*employed' or 'I'm *not* in work right now.' Even saying, 'I'm looking for a new job,' is an improvement. It affirms positive action; it tells people what you are *doing*.

In social settings it's possible to turn the situation around and take advantage of the fact that someone has just issued an open invitation to tell them what you're about. They may be able to put you in touch with someone useful. They may even be in a position to offer a job themselves (but don't ask them for one – see Chapter 2). Think also about defining yourself in ways other than by using employment-based references. Although their question may well have related to work, they'll probably be just as interested to hear about your skills as a tarot-card reader or your exciting plans to travel overland to Uzbekistan.

Don't allow your state of employment or unemployment to be the only way in which you view your life. Making sure activities not directly related to jobhunting are integrated into the weekly schedule will help. Use the time to find out about:

♦ training courses (many are free or at reduced rates if you're unemployed)

♦ computers and how to operate new programs (useful to include on your CV too)

♦ other jobs you've often wondered about

♦ other countries

♦ new leisure and creative pursuits (which provide opportunities to network)

♦ self-employment (see Chapter 9).

Fate often has a strange way of working. Circuitous, unexpected routes can open up and take you where you want to be better than more direct means. Terry Wogan started out as a bank clerk. Actor Richard Wilson was initially a laboratory technician. Paddy Ashdown, MP, was once a company director – and was then made redundant. Comedian Vic Reeves spent two years as a pig farmer.

This isn't to say you'd better buy a pair of wellies just in case, but there is a danger of becoming too blinkered in your job search, of falling into unproductive routines, of missing out on new opportunities. The rest of the book will give you the confidence to make the most of *all* jobhunt opportunities and the reassurance that you'll get there eventually.

Most of Us Start Here

Monday morning: the remnants of breakfast are drying out on the rim of the cereal bowl, and a second pot of coffee is a tempting diversion. Almost anything seems preferable to the dull plunge into the world of the jobfinder.

But the day has arrived. Whether it is the time to move from being a student or a frustrated high-flier, from unemployed or under-employed, today is when you become a jobfinder. But where to look? How to start? Where to find that job of all jobs?

Most people think of doing one of two things: looking in the paper under 'Situations Vacant' or taking a trip to the local Jobcentre, careers office or Jobclub.

Generally women concentrate on 'Situations Vacant', perhaps because they tend to like the printed word more than men (they certainly read more books), and men drop by the Jobcentre.

Whichever route is first used by the jobfinder, two points are worth highlighting:

- it's important to search thoroughly through what's there

- don't rely on just one jobhunting method.

It's as easy to become blinkered with jobhunting as it is with any other activity which develops into a routine: open the morning paper, scan the ads – nothing; visit Jobcentre in the afternoon for the fortnightly signing-on ritual – nothing; wait for tomorrow's morning paper – nothing ... This can go on for months. And for the two out of every three people looking for work who use these methods, it is exactly this sort of routine they are in danger of falling into.

There are two ways of breaking out of such mind-numbing routines. First, the job advertisements should be read closely and carefully – decoded almost – not merely scanned superficially. It is essential they are properly understood. Second, there are other places to hunt; less obvious but all the more worth while as a result. If it takes initiative and determination to reach them, so much the better; the less vigorous competition won't bother.

USING WHAT YOU FIND

Although the primary aim of pursuing job vacancies is to unearth those you feel confident in applying for, there are additional ways in which to use the information you come across. You may not see the exact job you had hoped to find, but there are still a lot of other facts worth gleaning.

The challenge is twofold:

♦ to look out for the ideal job, but also

♦ to recognise the value of other information you come across.

What information is useful and valuable? Facts, names, addresses and contacts related to the target job, company, career, work environment – in fact, anything related to your own personal jobhunt. Do not trust yourself to remember the odd fact: write it down; cut it out; make a photocopy; and keep an organised record.

Vital details are easily forgotten. The creation of a structured personal resource file into which useful discoveries can be put is central to the strategy of making information work to the full in the hunt for a job.

THE PRESS

Even the pages of the 'Situations Vacant' advertisements – the pages to which the majority of people who are in search of work turn – have more to offer than a superficial flick through a favourite daily can show.

NATIONAL DAILY NEWSPAPERS

The temptation for us all is to stick to what we know. The daily newspaper, the one we always buy because we like the editorial/sports/horoscope, arrives on the doormat every morning and because we're looking for a job we turn to the 'Situations Vacant' as well and look through.

The problem here is that the regular paper may not be the best one for job advertisements for the type of work wanted. Result: wasted time, disappointment, frustration at the apparent lack of suitable jobs to apply for.

Each daily newspaper focuses on particular types of jobs on different days of the week. For example, the *Guardian* carries job advertisements related to the media on Mondays, while on Wednesdays it concentrates on vacancies in the public and voluntary sectors.

It's not feasible to buy every paper every day, so do some research to find out which paper is the best for your own needs by spending an afternoon in your local library. Check through a full week's back copies of all the national dailies. Note:

- ◆ which career section they focus on each day of the week

- ◆ how their coverage of the types of jobs you're interested in varies; one may carry only six advertisements, while another has six pages

- ◆ the level of jobs they advertise: are they unskilled, low-grade, first jobs, graduate-level, executive or a mixed assortment?

- ◆ look at *all* the different job-advertisement sections.

This last point can be important. See what jobs are carried in the sections which you might otherwise skip over. For example, although you're looking for jobs in information technology you may be surprised to find relevant advertisements in the media section. Vacancies carried in the secretarial section may offer opportunities for general administrative work which would give you an entry to a target company or career field. Similarly, if you're finding it difficult to find a suitable opening in your 'usual' field, there may be lots of ways to use existing skills in paid positions in the voluntary sector.

Jobhunting can be expensive, so make sure you buy only those papers which will give the best return for possibly limited funds. If you're near your local library, use its copies for jobhunting instead of buying your own. You needn't go in every day, as few jobs advertised in the national press have such a tight deadline for responses that a gap of a few days is critical. Plan to go in, say, twice a week and cover all the papers in which you're interested at one go.

Once you've identified the papers you want to consult on a regular basis, there are more opportunities to be had than just glancing through the advertisements:

◆ look through the rest of the paper, business pages included. Aim? To spot employment, business or other news and emerging trends which might have some bearing on the jobhunt. It can also provide useful information to feed the discussion at interview and give evidence of being in touch. Items to look out for:

• major new contracts

• expansions, new factories, relocations etc.

• results of surveys, opinion polls and consumer trends

• reports of skill shortages

• new product development and launches

• declining markets (could signal a necessary change of direction in the career plan)

Any news item which relates to the target career or company is useful. Make a note of it (we'll look at how to make use of it in Chapter 3)

- look out for *any* jobs advertised by target companies. Make a note of the recruitment manager's name and telephone extension and the company's address

- look out for the readvertisement of jobs you were interested in but for which you may not have had the exact qualifications or experience required. If they couldn't appoint before, you may be in with a chance – especially if you entice them with willingness to negotiate on the salary to reflect this

- look out for salary levels. You may have to negotiate your salary at interview, in which case you need to know what the going rate is to ensure that you neither price yourself out of the running nor sell yourself short

- don't overlook specialist employment/recruitment agencies.

The scan of the national dailies should also include Saturday 'weekend' editions and the Sunday papers as well.

REGIONAL PRESS

Papers like the *Birmingham Post* and *Northern Echo* have circulations confined to specific geographical areas. Not only news items but job advertisements tend to have a local flavour. If the target job is in an area served by a flourishing regional newspaper, use it. Order a copy if the region is not your home. If you're not sure which one covers the region you're interested in, go to your local library and ask to see a copy of *The Media Guide* (Fourth Estate) or *Willings' Press Guide* which list all regional and local papers.

The library is also a good place to have a look at back copies of the local regional paper. As with the national dailies, check through to find out if some days are going to be better for your particular jobhunt than others.

Remember to make use of every scrap of information in the rest of the paper which might usefully be added to your jobhunt resource file. Make notes of useful contacts, etc., just as you would if it were a national daily. Check out if the paper offers any additional jobfinding services; some do. The London *Evening Standard* jointly runs PeopleBank (see p. 16) on the Internet in collaboration with the *Daily Mail* and also organises an annual Job Fair in London each September.

LOCAL PRESS

Local papers tend to cover a much smaller geographical area than the regional press, normally towns or even just areas within larger cities. Other than in large metropolitan centres they're likely to be weekly publications, perhaps with an extra mid-week edition, but many cities have their own daily paper, often an evening one, such as the *Manchester Evening News*.

The benefit of these papers is that the jobs advertised in them are likely to be with local employers, within easy travelling distance.

The range of jobs can be surprisingly wide, from management posts through to unskilled vacancies, although few executive posts are advertised through the local press. With some advertisements it may be necessary to be quick off the mark, so make sure you know the publication day for your own local paper and where to buy an early copy.

Again, always be on the lookout for relevant news and the names, telephone numbers and addresses of recruiters in businesses which are, or might be, important to you. Make a note and put the information into the resource file.

RECRUITMENT PRESS

Relative newcomers to newsagents' shelves are newspapers devoted entirely to recruitment advertising, a sort of job-finder's *Dalton's Weekly*. Their advantage is that they collect together in one publication a large number of job advertisements from which to choose.

Some are linked to local papers; others are independent. Some are weekly; others less regular. Most seem to operate on a regional basis, so check out what's on offer at your nearest large newsagent.

TRADE PRESS

Once you are certain about the career or field in which you want to work, you should find there's a trade publication covering it. They range from *Nursing Times* to the *Bookseller*, *Broadcast* to *Police*. Although some are subscription only, many are available through newsagents – and may well carry advertisements for the job you're looking for. A large newsagent should be able to advise what's available. Don't assume they don't carry anything on, say, marketing and public relations if there's nothing visible on the shelves when you call in. If they don't stock the trade journal in question, ask if they could order a copy for you. Alternatively, scan through *The Media Guide* or *Willings' Press Guide* in the local library, which will give details of all relevant publications – and while you're there, find out which magazines the library subscribes to. Some libraries can be persuaded to subscribe to new journals.

It's important to read not only the pages of job advertisements but the news and opinion pages. They are a quick source of gossip, trends and hints about the profession – crucial real-life knowledge that no amount of training can provide. This could give you the edge with your applications and help you stay ahead of the competition.

Depending on the frequency of publication (many are weekly or monthly, others are quarterly), some will prove better trawling grounds than others for vacancies. Weekly publications tend to carry more because of the shorter time it takes for recruiters to see their advertisements appear, but don't let this put you off looking through the less frequent publications.

IN-HOUSE PUBLICATIONS

Larger companies often have their own magazines or newsletters, circulated free to employees and often on display in reception areas for visitors to read. Some carry notices of in-house vacancies.

If there's a company you're keen to work for, find out if they have an in-house magazine and see if you can hijack a copy from someone who works there – or enquire whether you might call in and pick up a current copy. They can only say no, in which case you'll have to work on networking your way to a copy (see next chapter).

OTHER PLACES FOR JOB ADVERTISEMENTS

VACANCY LISTS

Instead of, and sometimes as well as, advertising vacancies through in-house publications, large employers often produce regular vacancy lists which are circulated among employees. Local councils are a typical example; their lists are often freely available at the town hall or library and indicate vacancies in most departments.

Phone target companies and ask if they produce a regular vacancy list and, if so, whether you could be put on their mailing list. If they don't operate one, ask how often their list comes out and if you can pick up a copy from reception. If not, try to get a copy from someone who works there. Be warned, though: some vacancies on in-house lists are open only to existing employees.

NOTICEBOARDS

Perhaps they are less popular than they used to be, but some companies still advertise vacancies on boards either outside their premises, hoping to catch the eye of passers-by, or inside their premises in public areas – supermarkets often use this technique. Investigate too reception areas in multi-occupancy office blocks, which sometimes have communal noticeboards.

It might be worth your while to trek around local employers' premises and note which ones have display boards. Take pen and paper with you to make notes. If you find enough boards, you may want to schedule a regular tour among your jobhunt activities, or try to find someone who lives or works nearby who will agree to keep her eyes open for you.

Also check out noticeboards in:

◆ community centres

◆ newsagents' windows

- church/religious halls

- other local meeting places.

ON-LINE SERVICES

Gradually, these are starting to open up opportunities for jobhunters via the Internet. Types of service available are:

- databases on which to register your CV and jobhunt details; employers and recruiters look for suitable candidates through each register. The Institute of Management currently operates such a service for its members (01536 204222), as does the *Daily Mail* newspaper via its PeopleBank service. It is free to register on this: phone Freephone 0800 200220, or access PeopleBank via the Internet on:
  http://www.peoplebank.com

- database registers operated by commercial employment agencies. Reed Personnel Services has established an on-line service for graduates (see *Yellow Pages* for your local branch)

- on-line job-match services operated by TECs, like the one in London's FOCUS area, accessed via libraries and careers offices. Check out what on-line services your own TEC provides (contact number will be in your local telephone directory).

The Higher Education Careers Services Unit has a useful Web site called PROSPECTS WEB, aimed at students. Besides carrying live job vacancies for graduates, PROSPECTS WEB includes a database of some 1,500 potential employers, holding company information, how to apply and contact information. Visitors can reroute from it and link directly into the Web sites of employers like British Telecom and Marks and Spencer. The database also has search facilities by occupation, subject studied, type of employer and location. Currently vacancy details on PROSPECTS WEB change every fortnight. Find PROSPECTS WEB at **http://www.prospects.csu.man.ac.uk**.

For a wider choice of vacancies it is worth visiting the Web sites now being set up by the national daily newspapers (at the time of writing some are at more advanced stages in developing their Web sites than others):

◆ *Daily Mail*: see PeopleBank (p. 16)

◆ *Daily Telegraph*: the Electronic Telegraph carries 80 per cent of the jobs which appear in the newspaper throughout the week. Find them at **http://www.telegraph.co.uk**

◆ *Financial Times*: carrying the majority of the jobs which appear throughout the week in the newspaper, its Web site can be found at **http://www.ft.com**

◆ *Guardian*: the *Guardian*'s Recruitnet, launched in 1996, professes to be the UK's largest recruitment database. An additional facility, aptly called 'Earlybird', alerts jobhunters to suitable vacancies as soon as they come up. Find Recruitnet at **http://recruitnet.guardian.co.uk**

◆ *Independent*: at the time of writing the *Independent* was in the process of setting up its Web site to carry all vacancies which appear in the newspaper

◆ *The Times/Sunday Times*: professing to have 1,000 new subscribers a day, the *Times/Sunday Times* Web site carries the majority of vacancies from both newspapers. As with the other dailies, there is no charge to register, and once you have done so you are free to browse through the week's job vacancies or use the key-word search facility to identify jobs with, for example, a named company. See what they have to offer on **http://www.the-times.co.uk**

◆ other titles: specialist magazines are worth checking out to find out what facilities are available on the Internet that are relevant to your job-search interests. For example, the *New Scientist* carries advertised vacancies on its Web site at **http://www.newscientist.com**

More employers are catching on to the usefulness of the Internet as a recruitment tool. A growing number are setting up and operating their own Web sites, from Ford (**http://www.monster.co.uk**) to Digitext (**http://www.digitext.co.uk**); from recruiters Price Jamieson (**http://www.pricejam.com**) to volunteer organisation Voluntary Service Overseas (**http://www.oneworld.org/vso/**).

Type in the sector in which you are interested (for example, 'retail') to see which companies have sites through which to browse. Asda supermarket runs a Web page and has found it a successful way in which to recruit new staff, with potential employees sending their CVs electronically in response to advertised vacancies. This facility is not yet available on all Web sites.

For jobhunters an additional benefit comes from using the Internet as a research tool. Complementing information gleaned from other sources, a visit to a target company's Web site provides instant access to material which might otherwise take valuable jobhunting time to unearth or receive through the post, such as company reports.

If you are not yet 'wired' but want to take advantage of the opportunities to surf for jobs on the Internet, try contacting your local careers office. Some offer Internet access. A growing number of main libraries are starting to go on-line to provide access for members of the public (some of them charge a fee), while the current fashion for cyber-cafés offers another alternative – plus cups of cappuccino.

RADIO AND TELEVISION

Both local and national radio stations offer careers advice, especially around the times when exam results are announced. Programmes and reports can be extremely useful in giving quality advice and up-to-the-minute information about what's what in the job market. Some local radio stations also offer jobhunt support and operate job-brokerage services. These vary from station to station and from area to area. Tune into, or phone, your local stations, both commercial and those operated by the BBC, to find out what's available.

Television also offers possibilities. ITV's Teletext service has job-related pages covering:

- write-in advice pages answering employment difficulties

- an education write-in advice page

- basic information about government-provided jobhunt support – for example, Jobcentres, Skills for Training, etc.

- regional information about local TECs and details of the Prince's Youth Business Trust for budding entrepreneurs

- job advertisements, although at the time of writing many are for information-technology specialists only.

The 'Jobs and Courses' index on Teletext, p. 640, lists what is on offer. And for those interested in working for the BBC, its job vacancies are carried on CEEFAX, p. 696. Unfortunately, this is all it carries for jobhunters.

JOBCENTRES

Don't knock them. One third of men and almost a quarter of women jobhunters use Jobcentres as their main method of finding work. However, according to statistics from the Labour Force Survey, only 8 per cent of jobhunters found work through this channel (1993 figures, the most recent available at the time of writing – not a very encouraging ratio). Still, in 1994 Jobcentres claimed to have helped jobhunters fill over 160,000 vacancies.

It's worth scanning the boards – not all vacancies are for unskilled, manual work. Administrative, secretarial, sales and other jobs are also advertised, and there are details of vacancies across countries in the EU. Jobcentres are also the places to find out about government-run training courses and other help.

Since vacancies arrive at Jobcentres every day, the best time to telephone them is mid-morning (once they've sorted through the new vacancies) to check if anything appropriate has come in. Try to cultivate some sort of rapport with just one or two members of staff – often an easy way of making dealings with the Jobcentre more productive. It will help Jobcentre staff identify more quickly the kind of work that would be most suitable for you.

EMPLOYMENT AGENCIES

Employment agencies fill thirty pages in the London *Yellow Pages* alone. Many specialise in areas like catering or estate agency placements, insurance or executive language specialists. They are far from being the domain of temping secretaries these days. Although some do deal in temporary work placements, many others concentrate on finding permanent positions.

By law agencies are not allowed to charge jobhunters for finding work, although stories abound of less scrupulous agencies delaying payments to people on their books for unnecessarily long periods as well as trying to get money out of them in various other ways. Be wary of any who are not members of the Institute of Employment Consultants or the Federation of Recruitment and Employment Services. At the other end of the scale some of the better agencies offer free training and full employment benefits, including holiday pay.

CAREERS SERVICES

The Careers Service used to be for school- and college-leavers only. Things have changed. All jobsearchers are now allowed a look-in for careers advice and the use of its facilities. However, the job vacancies it carries are mainly first and second jobs. No referral from school or college is required – the service is open to the public. The Careers Service may also offer on-line facilities and specific help with such things as drawing up your CV (see Chapter 6). Addresses will be found in the local telephone directory or library.

Universities operate careers services especially for graduates and postgraduates. It's worth seeing what's available at your nearest university even if you didn't graduate from there, or don't have a degree at all. You may have to pay slightly more to access its services, but charges are very reasonable. For example, a five-day access card at the University of London is free to current calendar year graduates and £4 to others (£2 if you are unemployed). Full careers interviews cost £45 (£23 if you are unemployed).

Besides helping you to sort through career choices, many universities host employer presentations, have on-line facilities and carry job vacancies. The University of London, for example, produces a weekly vacancy list and a careers magazine which you can subscribe to (University of London Careers Service, 50 Gordon Square, London WC1H 0PQ; 0171 387 8221), so find out what's on offer at your nearest seat of learning.

LOCAL INITIATIVES

Besides the statutory and commercial employment services, there are also many *ad hoc* local initiatives which may be well worth investigating. Some may target specific groups of people – say, people with English as a second language, people with disabilities or women returning to work – while others exist simply to supplement the work of existing agencies in the area in helping people find employment. Your local library and town hall should list all of them.

Watch your local press for details of job and recruitment fairs – and go. Dress well (but not over-smartly), arm yourself with copies of your current CV (see Chapter 6), pen and paper and have your best smile and handshake at the ready.

YOUR STRATEGY

With so many opportunities for finding job advertisements it's easy to see how jobhunting can quickly turn into a full-time occupation in itself – as many people soon discover. But, to go back to the beginning, it is important to investigate as many options as you can to identify those which are going to be most fruitful in the light of your particular needs. Don't dismiss any of them until you've actually investigated them – it's best not to prejudge, to listen to too much media hype or to decide on the basis of what one of your friends thinks.

Once all the possible options have been researched, work out a schedule so that you regularly contact all the bases without running yourself ragged. A desk diary, planner or organiser will help and will make sure you don't forget or lose track of what you're supposed to be checking on and when.

With such a schedule 50 per cent of all the outlets that lead to employment will have been covered. The territory will be the most crowded but no serious jobfinder can afford to neglect it.

Network into Work

HOW MOST JOBS ARE FILLED

The jobfinder can sometimes feel rather lonely – buried in mounds of newspapers and with only the Internet and local librarian for company. And if the hunt for work goes on, it is easy to feel a little paranoid, to conjure conspiracy theories to explain the elusiveness of jobs.

In one respect 'conspiracy theory' may be an accurate description, for jobfinding is often about whispered messages and discreet exchanges of information. The reason? The most productive way of finding a job is by word of mouth, according to a Labour Force Survey in 1993.

This means that people most often find jobs through hearing about them from someone they know, someone who works for a company or knows someone who does.

It seems as if the 'old boy network' is as alive today as ever it was, except that it's no longer confined to an élitist group of individuals with a handful of public schools in common – or even confined to 'old *boys*'. These days networking is what everyone can do and, as surveys reveal, it is the most usual way in which to unearth the route into employment.

THE EMPLOYER'S VIEWPOINT

It's worth considering why word-of-mouth recommendations continue to be popular with employers and how to make this method work for you. It all comes down to time and money. To place an advertisement, send out and sort through application forms, then arrange and conduct numerous interviews constitutes a lot of someone's time – and a lot of money. Placing advertisements in the press costs. And then there may be hundreds of applications to sort through. Postage alone can be a financial headache.

And even if references are taken up, employers don't really know who the applicant is and what he or she is truly about. For all they know, they might end up spending the year's profits on hiring someone who turns out to be completely unsuitable.

So from the point of view of the employer, sitting there wondering how to fill a vacancy, it's easy to appreciate the temptation when an employee or someone else they know tells them they have a friend/contact/relative who might be interested: no costly advertisements, no need to interview streams of people and they're able to get the low-down on the potential recruit beforehand. It's bound to bring a smile to the face of any cash-strapped employer.

However, this method does have its drawbacks. The Institute of Personnel and Development discourages the practice – and not without reason. The danger lies in encouraging an incestuous, closed-shop situation which perpetuates any existing inequality in the market-place for jobs. For the employer it also means that the price of taking the easy route is paid for in not necessarily getting the best and most able person for the job, just the most convenient to hire.

But until legislation makes it compulsory to advertise all jobs on the open market, you may find that networking is the best option you have to find the job you want. Additionally it is a skill that is of value in many professions, since it is about developing a wide range of contacts and relationships to provide a personal source of information which might otherwise be difficult, if not impossible at times, to acquire. Networking is a way of generating your own professional support system.

THE CHALLENGE

However insurmountable it may feel, the challenge is clear: you have to start networking so that you become the person others think of when they hear about a vacancy. Networking isn't only for top-flight business executives or other star players in the upper echelons. It's a skill, some might say an attitude of mind, which anyone can adopt. It's also a jobhunting necessity.

According to Donna Fisher and Sandy Vilas in their book *Successful Networking* (Thorsons, 1996), 'Anyone you might want to meet or contact is only four or five people away from you.' This includes potential employers.

Another reassuring figure they quote is that the majority of people have somewhere in the region of 250 contacts. And if this figure seems unlikely when you normally struggle to find a dozen names to put on your Christmas-card list (we'll call the list 'exclusive'), try thinking beyond that: consider people you come into contact with, however casually. This includes everyone from your bank manager to the bouncer at your local club, from previous work colleagues to current partners.

So although the networking challenge may seem daunting, we take part in it in everyday situations, like when trying to find a car mechanic. Picking one out of the *Yellow Pages* can be hit-and-miss, some garages being better than others. The best way to find a good one is by word of mouth, so what most of us do is ask around for a recommendation.

Networking is no more complicated than that. You are probably already a past master at networking without even realising it. The challenge is to transfer this skill to jobhunting.

DEVELOPING A NETWORK

Despite the 'exclusivity' of your Christmas-card list, you're probably going to be surprised at how many contacts you already have. So before adapting and honing your networking skills, examine your networking possibilities so that you:

◆ have a clearer picture of who forms part of your existing network

◆ begin to see the possibilities and develop a networking attitude.

Having a network isn't enough on its own; it must be sustained and used to the full, systematically, if it is to be effective.

You may find yourself starting to make a mental list while you're reading through this next section, and eventually go in search of a pen and paper to write down all those names which keep popping into your head. But a scribbled list is not going to work. It is important to record all the contact details in a more efficient way. If you have a personal computer you can create a database. Otherwise index cards will be fine and, depending on your computing skills, can be quicker.

How best to organise the data is a matter of personal preference. Alphabetically by surname may appear to be the easiest, but as the network grows it will be progressively more difficult to remember a remote contact's name. Consider organising the records by location (where you meet people), by date, by initial contact (whom you networked through to meet them), by the name of the company they work for or have access to or by any other way that enables the contact's details to be accessed quickly and efficiently.

Begin the network at the beginning: family and friends.

EXISTING CONTACTS

This is the easy bit. Write down for each:

- where they work

- where they have worked in the immediate past

- previous workplaces with which they may have kept in contact

- any clubs, groups, societies or professional organisations they may be members of (and if you don't know whether they do belong to anything, ask – that is what networking is all about)

- who they know (socially and professionally)

- where the people they know work.

That in itself will probably produce a three-figure network.

More index cards will be needed once the list of all those people you know but *don't* send Christmas cards to is investigated, plus any people you've met in the past. This can include:

- former schoolfriends, however distant

- schoolteachers, including the careers teacher, even if you encountered him or her only briefly

- ex-college/university student friends

- club members and social groups

- people contacted through regular shared leisure pursuits

- members and tutors of any courses you've attended

- people in your address book and neighbours

- former work colleagues, including those met during vacations, weekends or other casual work periods: they may have moved on to work for other companies, have useful friends and family contacts or even be self-employed and in a position to offer work themselves

- local people working in related areas of work – from retailers who interact with sales reps and manufacturers to bankers who deal with small businesses and charities, to local councillors who mix with managers, contractors, administrators and the media. Be broadminded and flexible in approaching as wide a circle of useful contacts as possible.

The list isn't exhaustive. Think laterally about the places you visit, the people you see and who or what they might know. And every time you go somewhere make a mental note of the people you can include in the network, however fleeting the contact with them. You never know who might have the inside information that will prove invaluable.

WAYS TO FIND MORE CONTACTS

It is said that anyone within a metre of where you are is a potential candidate for networking. Unless you work in the Scottish Highlands, that constitutes a vast number of potential additions to your network.

Situations which lend themselves to spontaneous networking opportunities include:

◆ travel

◆ libraries

◆ parties

◆ other social gatherings

◆ queues anywhere, but supermarkets can be productive

◆ letters pages in newspapers

◆ waiting rooms

◆ community gatherings - fêtes, jamborees

◆ cafés, pubs and other eateries or watering holes.

It is important to be selective; not all gatherings are appropriate, but it is surprising how many offer good opportunities for useful introductions.

Besides these day-to-day opportunities for starting to expand the network there are additional ones waiting to be explored through other channels:

◆ workshops and courses

◆ seminars

◆ presentations

◆ open evenings

- trade shows

- joining a professional organisation.

And in more structured settings the following can provide inroads to what might be invaluable contacts:

- work experience – although people think it applies only to students, there's nothing to stop you from writing to an employer and setting up a placement yourself; an excellent way to force a foot in the door

- work shadowing – similar to work experience, but the aim is to follow employees around and see what their work involves. For example, shadowing a sales rep while he or she makes calls on clients could provide networking contacts

- voluntary work

- serving on a board or committee

- temping – assignments can, and often do, turn into offers of full-time, permanent work.

These suggestions should give you some idea of how to expand your networking list beyond what you might have initially thought possible. New opportunities arise all the time. Even e-mail now offers the chance to develop an additional virtual network to complement your face-to-face one. The important thing is to start meeting people, chatting and listening to them.

DEVELOPING NETWORKING SKILLS

Not everyone is a natural networker – most people think of themselves as shy, and few have innate confidence when it comes to meeting and talking to new people. Networking isn't about attempting to forge instant friendships and buddies for life. It isn't a succession of chat-up lines, or anything akin to it.

Neither is it about brazenly and clumsily asking someone openly for a job.

Be clear about the aims of networking. The objective is informed advice. Those expecting to get a job just because they have asked for one will be disappointed – direct requests for work will generally be turned down flat. By contrast, most people like to have the chance to talk about their profession or company. It is flattering to be asked for one's opinion. And questions phrased in these terms will yield the best results – the best results being up-to-the-minute information that gives clues and guidance that might develop into an opportunity for work.

Networking might include any of the following approaches:

♦ to take an interest in people's lives and what they do, to foster good networking relationships for use in the future

♦ to find out who they know or to ask if they know someone in particular – e.g., the course delegate from a particular company who may provide an introduction to the person who hires staff; or the club member who may know the name of the person who runs the target business

♦ to glean information about a particular business, work environment or business sector – 'gossip' is another word for it – from opinions about overall company strategy or the health or otherwise of the market, to hearing about management's dissatisfaction with an individual member of staff, which could signal an opening

♦ to let people know what you do, what skills you can offer and the sort of opening you're looking for – if you don't tell people they won't know to tip you off when a possible opening does come up

♦ to swap information and leads with other jobhunters

- to find out how vacancies are advertised in someone's place of work and if they'd be willing to let you know if something comes up

- to ask if they can help you obtain relevant vacancy lists/newsletters/in-house magazines.

A day at a trade show is likely to produce a different kind of information from an evening at a drinks party. A little advance mental preparation will help. If the right opportunity arises, one of your most valuable tools will be your self-statement, which says who you are, what you can do and what you are looking for.

THE SELF-STATEMENT

It's a good confidence-builder to have a punchy, succinct line at the ready instead of mumbling incoherently at the very moment when a chance arises to give a new contact some useful information about yourself. It is worth practising this – the self-statement should roll off your tongue effortlessly and flexibly. Adjust it to suit the moment or person to whom you are speaking.

That person could be in charge of recruitment or the boss of a small business, so if he shows a polite interest during the course of seemingly idle chit-chat, take the opportunity to make your self-statement and pull the conversation around so that you become the focus. It might go along these lines: 'I've just spent two years in the publicity department of a voluntary group working on a great campaign. Now I'm ready to build on this and move into the commercial sector.'

If the networking opportunity happens to be a gathering of publicists, adjust the emphasis of self-statement, focusing on the different styles and attitudes of the voluntary and commercial sectors, for instance. Merely to declare that you work in publicity is, in such company, not very interesting. Be ready to adapt what you have to suit the situation.

However, don't include anything remotely like 'I want a job. Have you got one for me? Can you help me get one?' This doesn't give people any valuable information about yourself.

It puts them on the defensive; it moves the conversation towards closure (they will almost inevitably have to reply, 'No,') instead of providing an opening link into areas for discussion which might lead to disclosure of further valuable information on either side.

Make your initial self-statement concise (ten seconds' worth) and clear. Practise saying it out loud until it sounds good. Record it and play it back to help you get it right. What looks right written down may sound awkward when spoken. Change it until you're happy with it.

Personalised business cards can back up your self-statement effectively. They make it easy for people to contact you; they act as useful reminders; and they give the impression of professional seriousness. Business cards aren't exactly fashion accessories, but even the most style-conscious tend to use them. If your budget won't stretch to printed cards, think about buying some blank ones from a stationer's to write your details on as you hand the card over.

Networking isn't necessarily an intimate business. Don't expect to have life-enhancing discussions of philosophical importance. That's not the point. Few conversations will last more than five minutes – if they do, it's not necessarily a sign of progress. The aim is to meet as many people as possible, so that by the end of the meeting you have a handful of names you'll want to return to. Don't worry about the attempts which fail; you're bound to come across some social dead ducks whether you're at a wedding or a workshop for wonderful people.

Networking among familiar contacts isn't too daunting, but new situations can seem pretty terrifying. Here, though, the potential pay-offs can be enormous simply because new territory offers new opportunities. It's worth getting to grips with. As long as the event isn't wholly inappropriate it is better to be courageous and to mix as widely as you can. Be flexible; keep your essential self-statement in mind; prepare in advance as far as you can to anticipate the nature of the gathering and go for it.

After each event make sure you spend time recalling the new people you've met or updating information on cards for existing contacts. If an opportunity has arisen to further a contact, no matter how oblique to your ideal job, don't pass over it.

And for some general mingling advice:

◆ a simple 'Hello' with a smile is often all that's needed to break the social ice

◆ being honest with people about not knowing anyone at the event or not having attended one before often wins people over. If they know others there, you might ask them to introduce you

◆ make use of name tags if they have been provided

◆ show an appropriate interest in people and be an active listener

◆ when it's time to move on, acknowledge the usefulness or pleasantness of having made contact with your new acquaintance and, unless they want to introduce you to someone else, simply excuse yourself to go to mingle elsewhere

◆ it gets easier the more you do it.

Often, networking is about investing in the future. It may be further down the line – perhaps after talking to someone for the third, fourth or fourteenth time – that it becomes clear how this person might be of help, and, of course, most of the time you'll be meeting people who may never be of direct help to your jobhunt at all. You don't know, until it happens, exactly which person, which contact has the connection or information that will ultimately be the key ingredient for your jobhunt. But one thing is for sure. The more people you network with, the better your chance of hearing by word of mouth about the job you're looking for or otherwise to get help with your job search. The more often you network, the more your chances increase. And the more you network, the easier it becomes, the more confident you'll start to feel, and the more successful you'll become at it.

Job opportunities, or any other for that matter, rarely beat a track to your door no matter how grand or humble that might be. But when you let people know what you have to offer and the sort of help you're looking for, people can start to give you a hand. It's by showing a keen interest in others that good contacts will be formed and from which goodwill follows close behind.

Networking is no more about job-begging than asking about where to find a pair of jeans is about begging for the money to buy them.

Networking is about forming good contacts in order to maximise your chance of being in the right place at the right time so that you hear about those vacancies which arise and are filled so quickly they never even make it as far as the boards in the local Jobcentre or classified sections in newspapers.

One final suggestion. Since there is no saying when you might bump into that key person, it might be wise to make sure you always look presentable. It could happen anywhere – a casual introduction, a chance tip-off which needs immediate follow-up, an unexpected meeting with a shop manager. It's not necessary to spend every waking hour in a suit, but be generally well-groomed, neat and tidy. Look after yourself – and be courteous to others. It may not be an angel you entertain unawares, but it could turn out to be a potential employer at some future date.

Alongside other jobhunt activities, it will be necessary to schedule time to keep in contact with key people in your blossoming network and to start attending as many events and functions as possible. With this new focus and with clear networking aims you might start to feel there's barely time in your schedule for your existing job or even to sign on.

To Boldly Go ...

THE SPECULATIVE APPROACH

A reminder: the most successful way to find a job is by hearing about it from someone linked to the company where the vacancy arises. This is the way 30 per cent of people find work. After pursuing the advertised vacancies, the next most successful way to find work is by approaching employers directly, 'on spec', instead of waiting around until they place an advertisement in a newspaper, which you may or may not get to see.

According to the Labour Force Survey (1993), this method of jobhunting is what leads to success for 17 per cent of people – approximately one out of every six people, even though only 10 per cent claim to use it as their main method of finding work (International Labour Office, Autumn 1994). From these statistics it would appear that people who use, say, Jobcentres as their main jobhunting method benefit from supplementing their activities by making speculative approaches to employers. In the USA the figure quoted by Richard Nelson Bolles (*What Colour is Your Parachute?* Ten Speed Press, 1994) is much higher: it leads to success for almost half of all jobhunters. Perhaps this reveals a cultural difference. It may be that in the USA people are much more tolerant of the direct approach and fewer obstacles are placed in its way. It is perceived as a sign of initiative. Yet, if it produces such good results, perhaps we need to wake up to the more direct approach, especially while it offers a real competitive advantage over less adventurous job seekers.

THE BENEFITS

For the jobfinder, the speculative approach to employers can put you ahead of the competition straight away. It shows commitment and initiative – before an employer even begins to phrase the wording of the job advertisement. Indeed, their knowledge of a would-be employee might result in the vacancy never being advertised at all.

To be able to short-cut the time and expense of the recruiting process is always going to be attractive to employers. If they have your details to hand, you instantly put yourself ahead of other potential applicants who may end up waiting a long, long time to see the job advertised. With luck, you'll already be discussing a salary with your new employer while they are still scanning the vacancy lists.

Remember that approaching employers on spec should not be about begging for work but about presenting them with a neatly packaged solution to their problem of how to fill a skills gap left by an outgoing member of staff – as well as giving them something even better as a replacement. It's worth fixing the thought firmly in mind to help you adopt the right attitude to this jobhunt method. Be confident that you'll probably be someone's answer to a prayer.

If this approach is to succeed, it needs effort, research and the effective use of a growing network where at all possible.

WHICH BUSINESSES TO CONTACT

One reason why people limit a jobhunt to scanning the job vacancy advertisements is because it demands little effort: a trip to the newsagent's to pick up a newspaper, followed by a browse through what's on offer over a cup of coffee. Most people can cope with that. A job advertisement provides the relevant information about a vacancy, including the name of the business, where they are and who to contact. Some even provide a brief outline of the business's activities.

Approaching employers directly obviously demands a bit more effort because you have to find out all those company details for yourself. High-profile businesses might seem easy to investigate, but this is usually true only on a superficial level.

To get to know a company it is essential to look beyond the advertisements, glossy corporate brochures and PR puff (see Chapter 4). But large companies may not necessarily be the best ones to concentrate your efforts on anyway. According to *Employment News*, '95 per cent of firms today employ fewer than twenty people' (May 1996). In other words, most businesses are small businesses. Although the 5 per cent of companies that employ more than twenty people include some very large corporations with thousands of employees, opportunities for work may be more generally available in small businesses. They provide a much bigger pool in which to fish for a job. The pool consisting of large companies of over 100 employees is much, much smaller – 0.5 per cent of all businesses (Department of Trade and Industry, June 1995). These companies, well known as they are, will be the target of many other prospective jobhunters.

This doesn't mean you should remove them from your list, but it does point out that small businesses in your area may be a better bet, and you may find something suited more specifically to your skills and experience than among the narrower selection of the big firms. It's also generally a lot easier in a small company to get to see the person who hires new staff – normally the boss rather than a divisional or department head or personnel chief who may have strategies in place to discourage speculative approaches. Knowledge of small, local enterprises, however, is probably limited simply because they generally don't have a high profile, don't have access to expensive advertising slots on television and are not wealthy enough to be visible sponsors or donors.

Here are some ways to help you start drawing up your list of businesses to contact:

- local newspapers – news sections; business advertisements; all 'Situations Vacant' pages to get business names, addresses and who to contact – the vacancy may be for a packer, but it still provides valuable company information for you to use

- business directories – local, *Kelly's Directory*, *Kompass Directory*, Chambers of Commerce; all these can be found in your local reference library

◆ trade press – which you may be consulting already. Now you can make further use of the company information contained in it

◆ national newspapers often carry vacancies for lesser-known companies. Send off for details of *any* job in a company which you think might appeal. It will often send out general information about the business which you can make use of in your own speculative approach

◆ the *Yellow Pages*, the *Thomson Directory* and other guides to local services. Larger directories helpfully arrange entries in such a way that you can conveniently turn straight to the sections which contain those businesses in which you're interested.

With the basic information about the company, the next step is to make contact to request a copy of its company brochure and sales literature. They will assume you're a potential customer and will be only too pleased to oblige. This will provide useful background information to help you make a more targeted approach.

FINDING OUT WHO TO CONTACT

To make an effective speculative approach you need to find out the name of the person who does the hiring. Otherwise, the approach could end up on the wrong person's desk – frustrating and not especially impressive to the prospective employer.

LARGE COMPANIES

In larger companies recruitment is normally handled by the personnel or human resources department, in which case you need to find the name of the person who handles job applications. For example, at the international food giant Albert Fisher Group the person who fields them is Personnel Director Chris Frost, while at Grampian Television it is the

Personnel Manager, Elizabeth Gray. Graduate recruitment is often handled by another person. At Boots plc recruitment is managed by the Graduate Recruitment and Training Manager, Dr Gillian Frodsham.

To find out who you need to contact, phone up and ask the receptionist or switchboard for the name of the person in charge of recruitment. It's that simple. If you draw a blank with the receptionist, ask to be put through to the personnel department. The staff there are much more likely to provide the name of the person you need.

If you are completely blanked, mail your letter to the 'Head of Personnel', topped with a 'Dear Sir/Madam'. If it is company policy not to give out names, then you're not going to be the only one they receive a letter from addressed in this way. But it means that if you can possibly find out who this elusive creature is, it may put you ahead of the rest. Use your network, local careers office and any other resources at your disposal, including the company literature you should have received. A spokesman from ICI stressed the importance of getting a name if you're making a speculative approach – 'Then you'll get past the sacks of mail and past all the others and on to a specific person's desk' – which is precisely what you want.

SMALL COMPANIES

With smaller businesses it's much easier. The person who hires is probably the boss, and you may already have their name from the literature you've received or from your initial research. If not, the process is the same – simply phone and ask for the manager's name or use your network contacts to help you:

- find out if they know *anyone* who works there

- ask if you might contact that person for the purpose of finding out the name you need, or

- see if they might ask their contact for you.

If you get the chance to speak to someone who works at the company you're interested in, try to turn the conversation to encourage them to give details about the person who does the hiring, the current state of the business and what it's like working there.

GOING IN PERSON

The prospect of a rejection is enough to deter most people from showing up in person to ask about a job. Yet in some types of work – sales, for instance – people do that every working day: they know that when they receive the answer 'No' it is rarely, if ever, a personal rejection. Customers may well turn down a salesperson's pitch – but that is exactly what they're turning down: the pitch. They are not rejecting the salesperson as an individual. They decline because of any number of other reasons, most of which will have nothing whatsoever to do with the person standing in front of them. It is with this knowledge that a personal approach to a company should be made.

So forget about unhelpful images of carrying a begging-bowl. Instead a jobfinder may find she represents the perfect solution to someone's staffing or other business problem because of what she is able to offer. An employer may have spent the last six months dreaming of just such a person for all she knows. Her particular mix of skills and experience may be just what is wanted and it is these, plus how an employer might benefit from the new recruit's likely contribution, which is what's really on offer.

AIMS

Part of being prepared is in knowing what you're aiming to achieve. Making a speculative approach in person can be with the aim of:

- picking up an application form and, while you're there, getting a feel for the place and helping yourself to any company literature you may not have already, including vacancy lists

- finding out if there are any vacancies in the specific department in which you're interested in working

- discovering if it's worth while keeping this company on your target list

- getting to see the person who hires staff for a brief exploratory meeting

- taking the opportunity to leave your CV with the right person, so that when a vacancy does occur later on they have your details to hand and a memory of your meeting with them.

It would be a fortunate coincidence if the perfect vacancy appeared just as you arrived for your on spec call. Generally, the vacancy will not exist. But that doesn't devalue the point of the visit.

The aim of your meeting, if you can get to see the right person, is akin to networking. It's a chance to share information and, with luck, establish some common ground between employer and would-be employee. In a more relaxed atmosphere than would exist in an interview it's possible to find out what the general situation is with the employer and the business while disclosing valuable information about yourself which will hopefully start them thinking about how they might be able to use you to help them run a more efficient operation, increase profits or otherwise play a part in making the company succeed.

PREPARATION

You may not get beyond the reception desk but be prepared for the unexpected: you may be instantly whisked away to meet the boss, who just happens to be looking for someone with the talents you have to offer. So play safe. Make sure you're dressed appropriately. This means being clean and well presented even if the type of work you're after is on the shop floor rather than behind a desk. You won't be expected to be wearing your best interview suit – an on spec call is more relaxed than that – but it's important to flatter the company. Take it seriously; be dressed respectfully and appropriately, so that you are well placed to make the most of your visit. It would be a wasted effort if the head of personnel had time to see you straight away but gave the thumbs down because you had thought to pop in while you waited for the engine oil to finish draining out of the sump. Also:

◆ have a copy of your CV ready

◆ have to hand personal details not included on your CV (for example, your National Insurance number)

◆ bring samples of work which may be of interest

◆ make sure you have a notepad and pen

◆ think of questions you want to ask and a list of points you need to cover

◆ keep the aim of the meeting clearly fixed in your mind.

WHAT DO YOU SAY?

To the receptionist
Be positive and direct – and smile.

Say, 'I'd like to see Mr/Ms Blank for a few minutes, please.'

The receptionist is likely to ask you what you want to see them about. Answer: 'I want to discuss possible openings in the company with them.'

You may then be asked if you have an appointment. Don't dissemble. Say: 'No, but I don't mind waiting if they're busy right now.'

If you are told that the personnel director or boss is unavailable unless you have arranged an appointment, reply, 'I understand, but would you just check to see if they're free' (make it a straight but not aggressive statement rather than a question). They may well oblige, or they may retreat behind talk of 'company policy' and so on.

If this is the receptionist's response, it is prudent to seem to accept it. Reply, 'OK – but I'd like to pick up an application form while I'm here.' Don't say anything else. Leave the ball in their court and be quiet while they work out how to deal with your request.

To the person you were hoping to meet

You've only got a few minutes, so you need to get straight to the point. Keep the smile and thank the person for seeing you. Tell them, 'The reason I wanted to see you was to find out about possible openings in your business.' Add here any bit of inside information you've come across like 'I hear you've just won a big contract with Russia' or 'I heard on the grapevine you're about to introduce a new computer system' or anything else relevant to your skills and expertise which the person sitting in front of you could be looking for help with. If you've networked your way there, you may want to mention the mutual contact, whether that be a person or an organisation.

Hand over your CV and use it to highlight your best points: mention your key skills and personal qualities – but keep it brief, to a few seconds. Don't waffle. Give specific, pertinent information and don't feel that you have to blather to fill in any pauses in conversation. Give them time to think and to appreciate what you are offering. Help the employer to home in on the key points which will be most valuable to them.

Allow them to take the conversation on from there, but make sure you keep an eye on the ground you want to cover. Ignore the temptation to sit back. This is an information exchange, and you want to emerge from it with the answers to the questions you have as well as making sure you get across key information about yourself.

If you sense that the conversation is drawing to a close, don't attempt to prolong it. However, it's important that it should end as positively and directly as it began: leave a good impression. Be ready with your acknowledgement and parting shot: 'Of course, I realise it would be a bit of a fluke if there was a job just when I happened to call in, but what I'd like to do is leave my CV with you, if I may, and if anything does come up later on, perhaps you could give me a call.' Or you could ask if they have a vacancy mailing list your name could go on, or whether you could keep in touch by giving them a call in a couple of months' time.

Shake hands, thank them for seeing you and confirm that you hope to speak again in the near future (or whatever you agreed upon). Say *nothing else* as you start to leave apart from the final goodbye.

You've set the ball rolling with this employer – and now it's on to the next one. And the more you do this sort of thing, the more confident you become as you realise that:

◆ most people are pleasant and value the opportunity of having someone present themselves who may have just what they've been looking for. The occasional encounter with the odd grump or two is to be expected, but don't despair. Would you want to find yourself working for them anyway? Count those experiences as close shaves and heave a sigh of relief.

◆ these meetings really are about exchanging information in the hope of finding some common ground and not about begging for work or personal rejection.

Afterwards, and as soon as you can before you speak to anyone else, jot down a few notes about the meeting. Add them to your card-index file when you get home. Make a note in your diary of any action you agreed to take. If appropriate, quickly follow up the meeting with a brief letter thanking the person for the opportunity to meet them.

SPECULATIVE APPROACHES BY PHONE

You may be tempted into thinking that picking up the phone to make a speculative approach is easier than going to meet an employer in person. In fact, it's easier only for the person who answers the phone – easier to put you off, that is, and to put the phone down.

Trying to sell yourself to a potential employer over the phone is not a good idea. You may catch them at a bad time, so they'll say, 'No,' just to get rid of you. Even if they do have a vacancy, they won't offer you the job there and then.

But the telephone is still of use in your jobhunt:

- to request an application form

- as a follow-up to written communication (see next section)

- as an agreed follow-up to a previous meeting (see above)

- to request recruitment literature or a vacancy mailing from large companies

- to follow up a specific lead from someone in your network, either about a vacancy or to make contact with someone you've been recommended to speak to, possibly the person who hires.

When communicating by phone it is even more vital than when arriving in person to have a clear sense of what needs to be said, backed up by a script if necessary. This is what professional telesales people use to take them through their cold-call routines over the phone.

First, decide what your aim is in phoning. Then work out what you need to say beforehand. Write it down. Read it through, *out loud*. If possible, record it and play it back to hear what it sounds like and to get the intonation right. Change any words or phrases you find yourself stumbling over. And practise a few times until you feel confident.

- 'Hello. I was wondering if you could send me an application form/your recruitment literature.'

- 'Hello. It's Vince Vega here. I called in to see you a while ago about possible openings, and you said I should give you a call this month.'

- 'Hello. My name's White, Peter White. I was talking to Al Green the other day, and he said I should give you a call about the vacancy which is coming up in his section.'

◆ 'Hello. My name's Rose Arquette. I was talking to Mia Wallace the other day. She's a member of the same business group as yourself. She suggested I give you a call because she thought you might be interested in my particular skills and talents. I wondered if we could meet for a few minutes.'

If you're phoning to set up an interview, be prepared for them to ask when you were hoping to come in. Don't be caught off guard and blurt out, 'In ten minutes' time.' Have a bit more composure than that. Instead, suggest a time but make it flexible: ask how next week looks for them. Once you've agreed a day, be ready to suggest a time too, in case they bat the ball back into your court again. Say, 'What about 10.30?' If they mumble about it being a bit difficult at that time, ask when would suit them – be positive but not too pushy.

Once the time and date have been agreed, there's nothing more to be said other than that you'll look forward to seeing them. Don't start twittering on about how to get there and which bus to catch. Those details can be sorted out later. A prospective employer won't want to be bothered about resolving your travel problems; it will not impress if you don't seem able to work them out for yourself.

WRITING 'ON SPEC'

This method can be one of the most costly and time-wasting – or one of the best. According to ICI:

Don't just send a CV and a letter saying, 'I'm looking for a job.' We get lots of those. Sending out a general CV is like buying a lottery ticket.

We are interested in letters specific to the type of job an applicant is looking for in a location which interests them. Read the company literature and use it to help you target your letter – and make sure it goes to a named person.

You need to say exactly what type of job you're interested in and what you can offer the company, what skills, experience and personal qualities you can bring, such as leadership and commitment.

So covering letters need to be specific to each company you're writing to; outline what you can offer and how the company might benefit. All this should be conveyed on one side of paper:

- paragraph 1: why you are writing and what you are looking for. 'I read in the *Morning News* recently about your immediate plans to open a new office to serve residents in the north of the borough. Since this may create new openings for people with a keen knowledge of the local area, I thought I would contact you.'

- paragraph 2: what you can bring to the company – that is, why they should be interested in you. 'As a recent graduate specialising in marketing and PR in rural areas, my skills may be relevant to your new plans. In particular ... ' (here give a brief, itemised list of pertinent skills, achievements, knowledge, etc.)

- paragraph 3: closure and a proposal to follow up with a telephone call. 'I am totally committed to the ideals to which your company aspires and which are reflected in its focus and concern about community involvement. I feel I could bring the drive and energy needed to help make the launch of your new office a resounding success, and will telephone you next week to see if we might meet to discuss things further.'

Type your covering letter, send it with your CV and make a note in your diary of when to make that follow-up call. Should they agree to a meeting (and there's a one in three chance they will), you will need to prepare yourself as if for a job interview. It may turn out to be simply a networking event where you exchange information. You may not even find any common ground. On the other hand, you may find that after discussing in detail their needs, what you could bring to the company and how they might benefit, a job offer comes up as a direct consequence.

SUMMARY

For speculative approaches to work:

- ◆ find the name of the person you need to contact

- ◆ use your network to help and to find out essential background information

- ◆ consider the speculative approach as a way of building your own personal employment network, through which you will generate enough good contacts with employers for offers of work to come your way eventually

- ◆ target your enquiry to the company's aims as specifically as you can

- ◆ be prepared, and be sure of what you aim to achieve from any contact you make with an employer.

Jobhunt activities, network building and speculative approaches cover the avenues which lead nearly three-quarters of all people in the UK into work. Get the approach right and the odds of gaining the right job will shift substantially in your favour.

Should I Apply? Decoding Job Advertisements

Approximately a quarter of people in work find themselves there as a result of answering a job advertisement, and about a third of people use it as their main jobhunting method. Job advertisements, though far from giving the whole picture, clearly need to be examined carefully. To make the best use of them, save on time-wasting efforts and otherwise avoid being given the run-around by employers who should know better, it is necessary to know how to sort through the swathe of advertisements which face us on a daily basis.

WHY EMPLOYERS ADVERTISE

On the face of it, it may seem to be a bit unnecessary to look at why employers advertise. They do it because they have a vacancy, don't they? By law, yes: all job advertisements must be for genuine vacancies. But it's worth considering what else may lie behind their appearance:

♦ an employer may have tried other ways of filling the vacancy but has failed – it could be a particularly hard-to-fill position if the company is prepared to spend money on advertising it; if so, you need to find out why

♦ local people who know the company, its management and work environment may also know that it's a far from ideal employer

♦ company policy may dictate that it has to advertise

vacancies on the open market, even though an internal
candidate is already in the running

◆ employment agencies may place an advertisement for
an already filled vacancy and use it as bait to draw in
new clients – even though it is against the law to do so.

This isn't to say that all advertisements you see are suspect
– far from it. Open recruitment means that employers provide
the opportunity for anyone with the necessary skills, experience and qualities that the job requires to apply in fair and
equal competition with other jobhunters. But, it pays to scruti-
nise a job advertisement extremely carefully and to do some
background research on it through your network or other
sources if you possibly can.

EXPLICIT REQUIREMENTS

In an advertisement an employer has a very limited amount of
space in which to spell out what a job's about and what sort of
person they're looking for in order to fill the position. Sometimes they attempt to squeeze all this into as few as ten words:
SHOP MANAGER. FULL TIME IN LOCAL DIY STORE. EXPERIENCE
REQUIRED.

Not much to go on there, not even salary, but if it's the sort
of position you've been looking for and you fulfil the selection
requirements (meagre though they are), you'll no doubt want
to follow it up – and ask lots of questions later.

This is what advertisements can tell you:

◆ job title and level (trainee, supervisory, etc.)

◆ company information (what it does; its aims and ethos;
its size – employees/turnover/number of sites; building
design, if of note; characteristics of work environment;
its customers; other staff)

◆ location

◆ job content (this won't be a full job description)

- whether training is offered

- benefits (car, bonuses, holidays, lunches, discounts, company facilities, pension scheme, etc.)

- who you report to

- salary

- date when the job will start.

Then there are details about what the job demands and what the employer is looking for:

- academic or professional qualifications

- level of experience

- age – although employers are being strongly encouraged not to discriminate on this basis

- personal qualities (highly motivated, team worker, etc.)

- personal skills (good communicator, well organised, etc.)

- working background

- specific knowledge or expertise

- target groups (jobsharers, for example).

Finally there is information about how to apply and, possibly, an application deadline and a recruitment schedule.

That's a lot of information for an advertisement to carry, which is why it's quite a skill to craft good ones which attract the right applicants in the right numbers.

READING BETWEEN THE LINES

Equal opportunities legislation has meant that the subtle discrimination which used to appear in job advertisements has now been wiped out. However, there are still a number of coded messages which signal that an employer is looking for a certain individual. If you pay no attention to such implicit requirements, you could waste a lot of valuable time and money on applications which are destined to go nowhere. Conversely, you could miss out on an opportunity to match your skills and experience to the job's requirements. It's impossible to decode accurately one line of an advertisement when taken out of context. Indeed, often two quite opposite readings are plausible. That is why the additional knowledge gained by networking and speculative enquiry is so valuable.

'We seek a versatile person ... '

Is variety the spice of life or is this a job for a jack of all trades offering mastery of none?

Yes. If you can demonstrate your ability to turn your hand to a wide range of tasks, the sort likely to occur at the company which is advertising, *and* you like the sort of job which would demand that of you, then go ahead.

No. You may be asked, and expected, to carry out any number of chores, possibly outside normal working hours, and end up feeling like a general dogsbody in a deadend job.

'The chance to build a steady income ... '

If it can be built – increased – can it also be diminished? And should it need to be 'built steadily' if the income from the job is secure, and at a reasonable level to start with?

Yes. Taken from an advertisement for, for instance, tele-sales work, the wording would indicate you'd probably be hired on a commission-only basis. If you're already good at telesales, this is fine.

No. The rest of the advertisement might use a lot of language to convey the message that untold wealth can be yours but mention nothing about the job, other than that it involves talking on the telephone. The important word here is not 'chance' or 'steady' and certainly not 'income'. It is 'build', since this implies that you may earn a zero wage (literally no pay) until you manage to make a few sales – which, with or without training, can be pretty hard work at the beginning.

'The post demands flexibility ... '

Yes. 'Flexibility' is a buzz word employers now like to use. It can refer either to the hours they want you to work or to the tasks they want you to do. As with 'versatility' above, if you can demonstrate in your application that you are flexible and you enjoy the sort of chop and change it might imply, then go ahead.

No. As before, if the flexibility 'demanded' is a thin cover for the duties of a dogsbody at the beck and call of the boss's whims, then this should be read as a warning to all but the masochistic.

'An ability to communicate well with people ... '

Yes. Although the advertisement might not specify this, the work probably involves dealing in person with members of the public or with a wide range of employees from other businesses whom you may never know well. If you enjoy working in close contact with customers or suppliers and communicate well with people, it wouldn't pose any problems.

No. Being able to rattle on to friends about the latest gossip is not what is being asked for here. Although the job may be in a company you're interested in, if you don't enjoy being in the front line and dealing with all sorts of different people – perhaps in combative or aggressive situations – this post wouldn't suit you.

'Experience in the following is desirable ... '

Yes. If you can demonstrate experience in the areas listed, your candidacy will be viewed favourably. The employers are hoping beyond hope they can find that experience in someone but might be persuaded to settle for less. Even if you don't have all the experience, you should still continue with the application.

No. If you don't have the experience and yet are successful in getting the job, you may be thrown in at the deep end and left to cope. If you're called to interview you need to check what training they would provide or how central the experience is to the job.

'Must have initiative ... '

Yes. You could be left to work on your own unsupervised. The work is probably not a set number of tasks; you are more likely to need to respond to a changeable situation or workload and deal with whatever comes your way. This phrase is often used by small companies which don't have enough staff to offer full-time supervision and where the job may involve regular contact with customers or clients. If you like thinking on your feet and enjoy the responsibility of making decisions on your own, then you'd probably be happy in this sort of post.

No. The words may imply that you'll be left to muddle through without adequate training or support. Irregular feedback or poor management backing can lead to low job satisfaction. This needs to be investigated further.

'Young, go-ahead company ... '

Yes. This could mean the company is new, a real fledgling. The bonus of working for new enterprises is that if they take off, there's often a good chance to progress rapidly in line with the growth of the business.

No. It could also mean they have big ideas – and not much more – and that management and leadership skills based on sound experience may be lacking. The company may appear to be an exciting one to work for, but at interview, and preferably before, you need to check out what the management is like, how secure the company is (many businesses fold soon after start-up) and how others enjoy working there before you find yourself in a sinking ship which drags you down with it.

With so many job advertisements to scan through it's easy either to overlook the importance of key phrases which reveal a lot about the job or company, or to be taken in by enticing words and phrases like 'turn dreams into reality' ... 'warming to the task' ... 'time for leisure activities' ... 'security', which all appeared in one advertisement trying to lure people into sales work.

It's also easy to overlook advertisements for excellent jobs which are poorly designed and which your eyes skim over in the rush to scan more exciting displays. The style of an advertisement does reflect on the company: if serious about recruiting, a company should ensure its advertisements imply the importance it attaches to its employees. But there can be a gap between style and substance.

Sometimes poor design has nothing to do with the employer or the job but is the product of the newspaper's design department to which it was entrusted. Give your full attention to reading through advertisements and take a break if you feel it wandering, otherwise you'll notice important ads only when you are about to bin a newspaper.

It can be revealing to assess the relative weight an advertisement gives to job description, requirements and benefits. If it's a fairly hum-drum position, you may find more emphasis on selling the benefits which come with the job. Look out for waffle about how wonderful the job is that doesn't state anything specific about what is required and what the remuneration package is like. Screeds about requirements may indicate an employer's unrealistic expectations, which don't match the needs of the job.

JOB DESCRIPTIONS

The relatively small space filled by each job advertisement is a fairly basic sales board: it has to sell the job to interested potential 'buyers' (in other words, jobhunters), to grab their attention in the face of competition from other advertisements.

With such limited wordage at their disposal, many employers draft job descriptions. Although used primarily in the recruitment process, they also serve an important function in, among other things, making sure both employees and managers understand what is and isn't within the remit of the job.

Job descriptions give a much fuller picture than advertisements: what you see in a job description is what you get in the nine-to-five reality. Job descriptions are, or should be, detailed, specific, accurate and cluttered by none of the flowery hype sometimes found in advertisements.

Typically a job description contains the following:

- the full job title: this will have appeared in the job advertisement, although it may be expanded in the job description

- your line manager: the person to whom you would be directly responsible and who would oversee your work

- line-management responsibilities: the job titles of any people you in turn would be responsible for managing and supervising

- role: the aims of the job

- the job tasks and functions: what follows will be an itemised list of the main duties and responsibilities specific to the job in question; it will expand on key points covered in the job advertisement.

The job description is a vital tool in helping to understand fully what the job entails. Employer and employee might have entirely different ideas about what being a marketing assistant, for instance, entails. Without studying the job description carefully it is easy to waste time on an inappropriate application or, worse perhaps, to end up in the wrong job.

Not all employers refer to job descriptions in their advertisements, but there's nothing to stop you from contacting them and requesting one. If no formal job description is available it will be important at interview or in a preliminary phone call to ask the questions that will allow you to piece one together.

If a job description is made available, study it *very* carefully. Look at each duty and responsibility in turn. Then look at your own skills and experience and decide whether they match and therefore whether you could do the job satisfactorily. This is no more than the recruiters will be doing with your application and at interview.

PERSON SPECIFICATIONS

Another form an employer may send out is a person specification. It serves a function similar to that of the job description in

JOB DESCRIPTION
MANAGER: BRANCH

JOB PURPOSE
Plan and lead all aspects of branch performance to achieve the Society's business, financial, customer service and quality objectives for the branch.

KEY SKILLS REQUIRED
- Previous management/supervisory experience in a customer servicing environment.
- Good communication, planning and organisation skills both written and verbal.
- Decision making and delegation skills.
- Ability to manage resources effectively.
- Good knowledge of the Society's products, system processes and policies.
- A knowledge of competitors' products.

PRINCIPAL ACCOUNTABILITIES
1. Plan and agree performance criteria for the branch and its management team in order to deliver the branch's customer service, revenue generation, cost management and quality objectives.

2. Communicate the branch's plans and objectives to all staff in a way which gains their understanding and commitment.

3. By the use of Performance Management and other relevant management processes, continually review all aspects of branch performance to ensure the agreed objectives are achieved.

4. Through the branch management team and by personal involvement, ensure the highest standards of customer service are maintained at all times for all aspects of customer contact with the branch and supporting administration.

5. Provide coaching, motivation and leadership to the management team, and with them to all staff, to achieve the branch's objectives.

6. Personally lead the implementation of change within the branch, role modelling the required behaviours so that all change initiatives are implemented effectively and on time.

7. Lead the personal training and development of the management team and, with them of all staff in the branch, to meet both short term objectives and the longer term needs of both the Society and the individual.

8. Allocate and manage all branch resources, eg staff, budget etc to optimise business objectives.

9. Analyse and understand the local marketplace in order to maximise and facilitate business opportunities through the most appropriate channels eg Area Intermediary Manager.

10. Build and maintain relationships on behalf of the Society within the community, with key customers, agents and local introducers/influencers, to achieve business development objectives and project a positive public relations image.

11. Work with representatives from other group companies to maximise business opportunities and enhance customer service.

that it expands on what will have been mentioned only briefly in the job advertisement – the sort of personal qualities desired – and will form an important part of the selection and interviewing process.

A person specification may contain the following:

◆ academic qualifications required

◆ professional training which the person must have undertaken

◆ experience: this may refer to a particular work environment, familiarity with equipment, dealing with a particular client group, experience of a particular country, management experience, etc.

◆ abilities: the skills needed in order to do the job successfully. These may include practical skills (like the use of data-processing equipment) as well as management skills (such as an ability to prioritise work)

◆ knowledge: prior knowledge which is needed in order to do the job. The level required may also be stated, such as having a working knowledge of specific procedures related to the job

◆ personal: any personal qualities which are essential in order to do the job. These may include anything from an ability to deal with children to meticulous attention to detail, as well as more mundane matters like whether you can drive.

As with the job description, the person specification is a vital tool in helping you (a) decide if you're the right person for the job and whether you should continue with the application; (b) make a strong job application by pointing out how well you match the requirements of the job.

Study the criteria carefully. If you can satisfy each item,

you're well away and should proceed confidently with making an application. Even if you don't match all of them, you may still be in with a chance. Some lists distinguish between 'essential' and 'desirable' criteria. If you fulfil all the 'essential' ones, go ahead. If you don't meet any, it's unlikely that you'll be considered, even if you can match all the 'desirables'. And if you fit all 'essential' and 'desirable' criteria, the likelihood is that you will at least be called to interview.

With these documents, the job description and the person specification, employers lay their cards on the table. They declare what the job encompasses, the sort of person they want to recruit and their priorities in making the selection. Most employers will make this information available; some will have to be asked and may not have documentation. But they should be prepared verbally to tell you what person specification and selection criteria will govern their final choice of employee.

They've been honest with you. Now you have to be honest with yourself about whether you can do what the job requires, and want to, and whether you truly have what the employers are looking for. If you can lay hand on heart, you're in with a good chance. If not, it's best to accept that your chances of success are less than good. Your time may be better spent in setting aside that particular application and concentrating your efforts on other job leads.

FRINGE BENEFITS

Many employers include a full description of fringe benefits in job advertisements and recruitment literature. Some are pretty standard like holiday entitlement and pension schemes.

The benefits offered can help you decide whether to apply for an advertised post. Employers know that good fringe benefits not only attract applicants but also provide an incentive for staff to stay in post.

It's worth working out the value of the fringe benefits: according to lifestyle or personal circumstances, some benefits may take on more, or less, significance (access to company sports or leisure facilities or staff discounts could be important factors).

FILLING OUT THE PICTURE

However much information you receive from a company, it always pays to glean as much background as you can. This is where your network can be of enormous help.

If the network doesn't deliver any inside information, consider whether an informal visit to the company would be appropriate. Some employers reserve visits for shortlisted candidates only, while others advertise dates beforehand. For example, a recently advertised post for a counsellor in an advice centre carried not only dates for the deadline for applications and for interviews but also the week in which informal visits could be arranged. Not all employers are so open; one London council positively discourages visits for fear that candidates might misuse the event by canvassing support for their applications. But if, because of the nature of the job, the work environment would be important to you, there is no harm in contacting the employer and enquiring whether a visit could be arranged. Don't be put off if they won't oblige. Companies that don't advertise visits may turn you down, so be prepared. Small businesses especially may not be able to accommodate visits simply because of work/time pressures.

If a visit is possible, take advantage of the opportunity to go and see for yourself what the business looks like from the inside. Make use of the 'guide' who conducts the tour: ask what it's like to work there and what the boss is like. Make a mental note of the following while you're wandering around:

- is the general atmosphere busy yet friendly or is everyone frantic?

- does it look well organised or reveal the origins of chaos theory?

- does the overall decor seem pleasant enough to work in day in, day out?

- what are the staff facilities like?

- is it open-plan or is everyone shut in cubby-holes?

- is it easy to get to?

- as a visitor, are you treated well?

A brief visit is well worth the time and effort. It gives another chance to assess the appropriateness of your application as well as providing additional information which may be useful later. The familiarity provided by the visit is a useful boost to confidence at interview. Every bit helps.

DO I PROCEED?

Success at jobhunting takes more than routine scans of advertisements and applications by the truck load.

- make sure you read advertisements carefully – very carefully

- think about why the employer might be advertising the post

- make sure you understand any hidden messages in the advertisement – if you're not sure, ask someone else to read it through

- use the job description and person specification as tools to help you decide whether to proceed

- consider whether the fringe benefits have any bearing on your decision

- use your network contacts to help you decide

- try to arrange a preliminary visit to a prospective employer. Seeing is often believing.

Your time, energy and resources are precious. Find the balance between being too critical and too enthusiastic; learn when to pull the plug on pursuing a job. The better targeted the applications, the better the chance of success in the right kind of work.

So You Want to Go Ahead? The Science of Applying

TYPES OF APPLICATION

Depending on the size of the organisation and the level and type of job, you may be invited to apply in any number of ways:

- turn up in person at a specified place and time – normally for casual, manual/farming work

- apply in person – small local businesses use this method, often for lower-grade or manual jobs

- attend a group briefing – often used in mass recruitment drives. Speakers address potential applicants at organised meetings and describe the work and the company; briefings also provide an opportunity for people to ask questions

- send for an application form or information pack – more common with larger, well-established companies, including local and central government departments and offices where recruitment is ongoing and procedures are standard

- send in your CV – popular with many employers now, although some still require a completed application form as well, to suit their own administrative procedures

- apply in writing – smaller firms often request letters of

application to help them fill clerical, middle or higher-grade posts

◆ apply by telephone:

• to request application forms; they may have an answering machine, set up specially to deal with requests, on which you leave your name and address

• used by some as an initial screening method, especially if the job you want to apply for involves telephone work or contact with customers or clients

• to arrange an interview; often used when employers need to appoint quickly for lower-grade, entry-level, sales or temporary work.

The most common means of introduction are application forms and covering letters, letters of application and applications by telephone, which we'll look at next. CVs are covered in the next chapter.

APPLICATION FORMS

For employers the application form standardises the responses to advertised vacancies, allowing easier comparison between applicants and swifter exclusion of unsuitable candidates. They look at the job description and/or person specification and match it with what they find on the application form. (The form on the following pages is reproduced by kind permission of Thomson Holidays.) Within the space of a few minutes an unwieldy pile of hopefuls can be cut back drastically. For recruiters it's quicker and more accurate than reading through letters and even CVs compiled in different styles with varying degrees of wordiness.

How well and accurately the form has been filled in is a test in itself. A careless or cavalier display is an early indication to an employer that an applicant may not be suitable for the job. Application forms can be irritating and fiddly to complete, but it is important to follow their requirements to the letter. Generally they are not looking for creative responses; save that for later.

THOMSON

Application Form

Please read this form carefully and complete it fully

Strictly confidential

Position applied for

Personal information

Surname:

Forenames:

Home address: Contact address (if different):

Home telephone number: Office telephone number:

Day	Month	Year

Date of birth: Nationality:

Do you require a permit to work in the UK: YES/NO

Do you have a current driving licence?:   YES/NO

Please give details of any motoring convictions with dates:

Details of any relevant condition or disability:

No. of days absent from work through illness in the last 12 months - please state cause:

If you have a disability are there any specifics facilities you would require at an interview if you were short-listed?

Notice period:

Education

Include professional education and qualifications in date order

School, College, University	From	To	Certificates, Diplomas, Degrees obtained Please give level of pass

Work related development/training

Please list courses/seminars attended in the last five years

Date (year)	Organising body	Title and purpose of event

Employment History

Present (or most recent) employment. Name / full address / business of employer	Permanent / temporary contract*	From	To	Current salary / salary on leaving	Main responsibilities and activities	Reason for leaving

Previous employment. Name / full address / business of employer	Permanent / temporary contract*	From	To	Salary on leaving	Main responsibilities and activities	Reason for leaving

*Please delete as appropriate

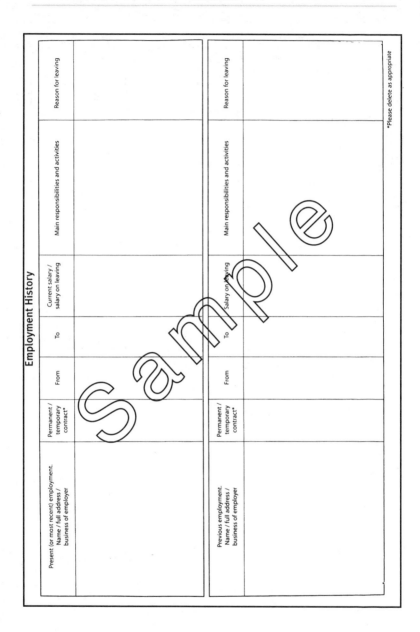

Outside Interests

Please give details of any interests and membership of any organisation, society or club

Additional Information

Please state your reason for applying for this post and include any relevant information in support of your application

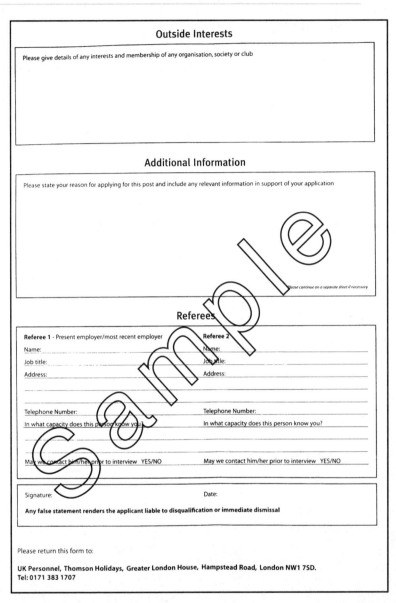

Please continue on a separate sheet if necessary

Referees

Referee 1 - Present employer/most recent employer

Name:

Job title:

Address:

Telephone Number:

In what capacity does this person know you?

May we contact him/her prior to interview   YES/NO

Referee 2

Name:

Job title:

Address:

Telephone Number:

In what capacity does this person know you?

May we contact him/her prior to interview   YES/NO

Signature: Date:

Any false statement renders the applicant liable to disqualification or immediate dismissal

Please return this form to:

UK Personnel, Thomson Holidays, Greater London House, Hampstead Road, London NW1 7SD.
Tel: 0171 383 1707

DUMMY RUNS

Only one application form will be sent – one chance to get it right. Lots of crossings out and amendments, no matter how neatly done or carefully 'whited out', can be one of the reasons why a recruiter chooses to eliminate an applicant from the proceedings.

To ensure a smooth passage through the first, cursory, level of screening, the application has to look good. Maximise your chances by:

- making a photocopy of the blank application form and use this for a first draft of the application

- keep within the spaces provided for the basic information

- If your handwriting looks like a design for a rollercoaster, place a sheet of lined paper underneath the form as a guide

- afterwards, read through and check your draft

- then get someone else to check through it – someone who can spell and whose grammar is good

- if there's time, put this practice form away until the next day at least, then look through it again with fresh eyes.

The last point is important. After working on a document for any length of time it's easy to become blind to mistakes.

Failure to follow simple form-filling instructions and to care about presentation is seen by employers as evidence of an applicant's inability to follow instructions on the job, tendencies towards error and a sloppy attitude that might well colour their work. It's a route to instant rejection. So the dummy run is important. But it's also important to transfer the information correctly to the real application form:

- consider using a soft-lead pencil (not a scratchy hard one that leaves indentations on the paper) to copy the details from the dummy-run form on to the real application form, which you will then overwrite in ink or as required

♦ use the lined paper again as a guide

♦ make sure you have the right type and colour of pen to fill in the form properly – some employers specify what they want

♦ if you are writing over pencil marks and erasing afterwards check that the ink doesn't smudge when you use an eraser; if it does, choose a different pen. And if the eraser leaves a grubby or coloured mark, get a new one that doesn't.

Good presentation has one simple objective: it allows the recruiter to concentrate on the content – what really matters – rather than the superficial distractions of errors and smudges.

FILLING IN THE FACTS

Most application forms are pretty self-explanatory; any special instructions about filling one in are normally given at the top of the form. Always read them.

The main sections will cover:

♦ personal details – name, address, etc.

♦ education and training – unless otherwise directed, start with the most recent

♦ employment history – the same goes for this section. Under 'Duties' include special responsibilities and achievements. Under 'Reason for Leaving', keep your remarks brief, to the point and honest. If you were sacked from a job, you probably weren't happy there anyway, so mention what you were dissatisfied with – poor line management, lack of challenge, an unsatisfactory relationship with your employer. If you were made redundant, word it that the *job*, *position* or *department* was made redundant. Stick the redundancy label on the job, not yourself.

◆ reason for applying – see below

◆ details of referees – always ask people if they are willing to act as referees before including their names on the form

◆ closing instructions – read them carefully because they may contain important information.

THE BLANK BIT

This is the section which floors most people. The instructions are worded variously and might be any of the following:

◆ 'Please give your reasons for applying for this post'

◆ 'Please provide a statement in support of your application'

◆ 'Include any further information in this section which relates to your application'.

This is your chance to shine, the moment to highlight all those important points that lie hidden deep in your employment history and personal development. This is the place to show just how well you match what the employer is looking for.

Wordiness is not what is required here. Instead give evidence that you can do the job and that you will bring the right qualities to the work. Bullet-pointed lists will be just as impressive as finely turned sentences.

If a job description or a person specification has been provided address each point in turn. The more points directly covered, the stronger the application.

For example, if the job description or advertisement asks for someone who has experience of Word for Windows 6.0, say:

In support of my application, I feel I am a suitable candidate for the post because:

◆ I have two years' experience of working with Word for Windows 6.0 on a daily basis.

If good communication skills are needed, include another bullet point that directly addresses the need:

◆ I enjoy working directly with clients in person and have recently completed a Communication Skills course to NVQ [National Vocational Qualification] Level 3.

Cover as many points as possible and include any relevant information which you want to ensure they notice. Don't be shy or modest, but keep it relevant:

In addition, I would like to highlight my involvement in successfully developing a more efficient work-scheduling system which resulted in a 50 per cent reduction in delays. Much of the planning work was carried out in addition to my normal range of duties.

A person who has the experience and skills demanded, and who has demonstrated a commitment to his career through the pursuit of a training course, and who can also show he works hard and is focused on a company's success should delight any potential employer. All else being equal, the next communication should be an invitation to attend an interview.

If there is no job description to refer to and the advertisement covers only the bare bones, use whatever information the visits or other sources have produced. Besides skills and experience specific to the job, most employers are looking for:

◆ a co-operative attitude – can you demonstrate you are a good co-worker?

◆ reliability – not just time-keeping: can you demonstrate

that you can be trusted to carry out agreed tasks to an agreed standard and respond to the level of responsibility the job may demand?

- ◆ commitment – can you demonstrate that your aim is to help the company succeed and that you are a hard worker?

- ◆ honesty – positions of responsibility both in and out of work will help to convey this message

- ◆ enthusiasm.

They are also interested in:

- ◆ your immediate career aims

- ◆ what motivates you – the kind of challenge that inspires your best work

- ◆ anything else of relevance which will clarify your attitude to work and how you might fit into their organisation, such as evidence of potential or actual leadership skills or preference for a particular kind of work environment.

If what you want to say won't fit in the space provided, attach a continuation sheet unless expressly told not to. Do make sure it is just the one sheet. No recruiter will plough through verbose applications – they ensure only that you are screened out.

Finally, before the application form is posted or delivered, read it through again and take a photocopy of it. At interview you will be at a disadvantage if you cannot remember what you wrote. So familiarise yourself with its contents again before the interview.

COVERING LETTERS

Assuming there was space on the application form in which to make your personal pitch for the job, the covering letter you send need only be brief. Something along the lines of:

Production Assistant

With reference to the above post, I now return the completed application form as requested.

Should you require any further information, please do not hesitate to contact me at the above address.

I hope you will give my application due consideration, and in the meantime I shall look forward to hearing from you in the near future.

If no space was provided on the form to make a statement in support of the application, then use your covering letter for the purpose. Draw the employer's attention to important points which focus on how well suited you are to the selection criteria, just as if the selection criteria were mapped out on the page.

The letter's first paragraph should be similar to the one above. Then use the rest of the letter to give your reasons for applying as outlined in *The Blank Bit* on p.70. Write it in just the same way, preferably on a single side of A4 paper, using bullet points to keep it brief and to the point. The second paragraph should introduce this section:

I would like to draw your attention in particular to the following:

◆   I have successfully handled, from design to publication, Happy Petfood's latest edition of its newsletter for customers.

◆   I have also . . .

End the letter in the same way as a cover letter accompanying an application form.

Use the same procedure for letters that are sent with CVs. Don't leave it to chance that the recruiter will automatically interpret what's on the CV in such a way that she instantly matches the application to the job. Instead assume the recipient of your CV is having a bad day. The covering letter should do the equivalent of standing over and prompting the employer, reminding him or her what the job requires and showing how well the information on the CV meets those requirements.

LETTERS OF APPLICATION

Many businesses aren't big enough to have their own application forms and are happy to accept CVs from applicants. Others simply request letters and ask only that people 'Apply in writing'.

Such a letter should include essentially the sort of statement that you might make in the blank space of an application form (see p.70). The letter affords more space; up to two sides of A4 instead of just one. Bullet points are still helpful in highlighting key points, but there is also room to expand information about training and work experience.

The objective is the same: match what the employer is looking for with what you can provide. Be as rigorous in checking off the core elements of the job as you would be in the more formal application form.

APPLYING BY TELEPHONE

If the job advertisement invites you to make a telephone call simply to request further details or arrange a time for an interview, it should pose no problems. However, if it is unclear what the phone call will include, it is wise to be prepared. Expectations of a dull conversation about application forms can quickly turn into an interview – and no interview will go well unless the interviewee is prepared for it. So be sharp and ready for any direction the phone conversation might take:

- ◆ arrange to use a private phone, not a public call box if you can possibly avoid it. If you can't, choose one in a quiet street and use a phonecard

- ◆ have your CV with you so you can answer questions about work experience

- ◆ make a list of points you want to make

- ◆ make a list of any questions you may have

- have a pen and paper to make notes

- practise answering interview-type questions about the job, like 'Tell me a bit about yourself' and 'Why do you think you're a suitable candidate for this post?' (see Chapter 7). Remember: keep your answers relevant to the job

- get a friend to role-play the employer if you can.

Applying for a job by telephone isn't the easiest situation to handle, especially if it's unexpected. Without direct, face-to-face interaction it is difficult to gauge the interviewer's mood and responsiveness. It is important neither to under-sell yourself and forget to mention important points, nor to over-sell yourself and allow a note of desperation to creep in. Preparation will help – as will thinking the interviewer as a constructive and potentially helpful ally who is trying to allow you to establish that you are the right person for the job and that they are the right employer for you.

The CV: Your Own Personal Advertisement

THE CURRICULUM VITAE: WHAT IT IS AND WHAT IT DOES

A CV provides in the space of one, possibly two, sides of A4 paper a summary of a person's education, training and work experience to date. That's the minimum it should contain, and a poor CV will tell you little more than that – name of school, college, place of training and a list of previous employers. A poor CV merely establishes a person's whereabouts over the previous few years – and that is not much help to a recruiter who needs to have substantial reasons for spending time on interviewing applicants. A good CV, on the other hand, conveys all the reasons why an employer should want to know more about the applicant. It excites interest by showing clearly that here's someone who can offer distinctive skills, abilities and personal qualities.

The essential aim of a CV is to interest an employer sufficiently to unlock the door to the next stage of the recruitment process. CVs alone won't get you a job, but they must beat off most of the competition, which for some jobs can be fierce. So although a CV is a summary of what you've been doing with your life to date, it also:

◆ serves as a vehicle to convey your relevant achievements and accomplishments

◆ shows how well you're likely to perform in the job you're applying for

- indicates what skills, experience, abilities and personal qualities you can bring to both the job and company as a whole

- indicates attitude, enthusiasm and other characteristics.

The CV is vital: it is your personal advertisement, created, directed and produced by you, and it may be your one and only chance with an employer. Although a good CV will be personalised it is important that the information is fully and appropriately laid out.

THE BASIC FRAMEWORK

PRESENTATION

Don't be rejected because your CV is shoddy, error-strewn or unnecessarily rococo in style. Keep it smart, straight and effective, and avoid:

- handwriting

- coloured paper

- photocopying

- photographs, unless expressly requested

- dense writing

- dog-eared edges – a sign that the CV has done the rounds

- needlessly decorative typefaces or fancy headings

- faint or smudgy script.

CONTENT

Personal details
- name, address and telephone number are sufficient

- if the advertisement specifies an age limit, include your date of birth

- centre these details or position them on the left-hand side of the paper.

Work experience

- start with your most recent employment

- state the period during which you worked for each employer (month and year); the reason for leaving is not normally included on CVs

- give the name of each company and its location (not full address)

- next put your job title

- on the next line itemise your main responsibilities and duties; give most details for the most recent employers

- it's essential to include those of your achievements and accomplishments that are relevant to the job you're applying for.

Although it may be tempting to leave out periods away from the world of work, employers like to see time accounted for; they treat gaps with suspicion. If two years were spent travelling abroad, say so. If appropriate, pick out relevant experience gained along the way, such as life in different cultures. Even a long period of unemployment should be acknowledged positively. If it has resulted in a career change, mention that the time has allowed you an opportunity to reassess your professional career path. Pinpoint what you have done to further new ambitions, such as following a training course or gaining unpaid work experience. (See also Chapter 7).

Jane Garrett
111 Laidlock Lane
London, W15 100
0171 001 9999

WORK EXPERIENCE

1995 – Present BLOTT & CO., LONDON W19
Assistant Reprographics Manager

- ensuring on-time delivery of all photocopying; 95 per cent success rate
- researched and recommended installation of MANTER 3100Z high-volume photocopier resulting in 20 per cent savings on costs
- organising equipment maintenance and repair
- improved existing reporting system, limiting average downtime from two days to no more than half a day
- daily recording of reprographics throughput
- supervision of two clerical staff.

1993 – 1995 J.D. REAM COPY SHOP, BRIGHTON, EAST SUSSEX
Retail Assistant

- customer order-taking
- recommended new order-form design resulting in 10 per cent fewer reported problems with orders
- advised customers on printing processes and relative costs
- operated DIGIS 115 photocopying machine and basic finishing equipment.

MEMBERSHIPS
1996 Reprographics and Design Association

EDUCATION
1991 – 1993 EURO COLLEGE OF PRINTING
HNC in Reprographics

Professional memberships, etc.

- note membership of any organisations recognised in your particular profession – just state their names

- include details of any special involvement or posts held

- include any other accomplishments relevant to your profession, such as special awards or distinctions.

Education and training

- details of any training or course of study since leaving formal education

- name of college or university and years of attendance

- qualification and subject

- if applying for a first job, years of attendance and name of school with subjects and grades

- years of attendance and name of school if no further or higher education followed

- don't include evening classes and courses attended for personal interests unless they are directly relevant to the job.

Additional information

- include skills relevant to the job you're applying for which haven't been mentioned elsewhere. For example, if it's relevant, you may want to include details of any computer packages with which you're familiar, your degree of proficiency in another language or whether you have a full driving licence.

Leave out

- names of referees – according to chairman Nick Hawkins at Interexec plc, this is the norm nowadays, as employers accept that applicants may not want to use the same referees each time they send out a CV

◆ hobbies

◆ statements about career aims

◆ anything else you might be tempted to put in but which isn't wholly related to the job. Remember: an employer may give the CV a glance of barely a few seconds, so all available space should be used to make an impact with information that is *directly relevant* to the post.

THE LANGUAGE OF THE CV

Not everyone is a budding Tolstoy when it comes to writing, but this won't affect the impact of a CV: the less wordy it is the better. Employers don't have either the time or the inclination to wade through eloquent but lengthy prose. All a CV should provide is a tailored list – and most people can do that. A well-focused and sharply targeted list of key points makes it easy for an employer to see what is on offer. It's the opportunity to highlight selectively from a full range of skills and experience in order to entice the employer. Don't mess it up by clouding the issue with waffle.

PREPARATION

On a piece of scrap paper jot down all that you do in your present or most recent job. Don't worry about the wording at this stage; just make notes. Include:

◆ tasks carried out on a daily, monthly or even yearly basis

◆ specific responsibilities related to staff, budgets, work environment, service provision, etc.

◆ job-related skills, such as use of specific equipment, computer programs, book-keeping skills, etc.

◆ involvement in special projects and the level of involvement

◆ achievements: involvement in company successes, personal accomplishments and progression – employers like to see results.

Rearrange the list, putting the most important statements first. Now look at the wording you've used. The bullet-pointed list you're aiming to produce for your CV should contain short, abbreviated descriptions and not necessarily full sentences. Follow these guidelines:

◆ omit 'I'

◆ omit as many other words as you can, like 'the' and 'that', unless they change (the) meaning or readability

◆ try to start each item with a verb – this makes the point that you're actively doing and achieving things in your work

◆ use adverbs to convey how the achievements were fulfilled. Instead of 'My responsibilities included training staff in new customer-care procedures' change to 'Successfully trained staff in new customer-care procedures'

◆ try to target, say, six main points. Edit out the less important aspects

◆ make sure what you're left with is directly relevant to the job you're applying for.

The aim is to end up with a concise list which sounds dynamic and well focused.

RESULTS WORDS

Employers like to see evidence of achievement. Prior accomplishments offer the promise of future benefits to them. These words say 'results' to anyone reading them:

increased	improved	successfully
identified	reduced	established
developed	initiated	negotiated
produced	launched	recognised
designed	motivated	co-ordinated
organised	saved	created
fulfilled	exceeded	surpassed

Sample bullet points:

- 'improved service to customers' instead of 'worked on customer service programme'

- 'negotiated better terms with suppliers, saving 15 per cent on costs' instead of 'dealt with suppliers'

- 'recognised potential for growth in new sector' instead of 'business development'

- 'established improved administrative systems' instead of 'clerical work'

- 'successfully devised and co-ordinated interdepartmental meetings initiative' instead of 'set up internal meetings'.

These phrases demonstrate levels of accomplishment and show what you are capable of achieving. Include as many words indicative of good results as you can. Putting 'new project manager' gives an indication of your role but more mileage could be gained with phrases like 'successfully launched new project' or 'quickly established effectiveness of new project'.

TAILORING YOUR CV

It's tempting to think that once the information on the CV has been compiled, it can be reproduced automatically for each application.

In some instances that may be possible. But before printing another copy from the word processor, remember that this is probably the one and only chance to impress an employer. So make sure the CV really sings to each individual recruiter it is sent to.

Examine the job advertisement and job description in particular, as well as the company details and any other information available. Look at what they're looking for specifically in terms of skills, experience and abilities. Now look again at your CV. Does it address the job requirements precisely? If the employer requires someone with experience of specific equipment, computer programs, processes or client groups, does the CV cover those details? If team-working skills are requested does the CV highlight them?

Don't presume that someone reading the CV will infer anything – spell things out. Make it easy to match the crucial elements.

If this means reworking your CV slightly for each application then do so. It is a valuable way to use jobfinding time. Without a computer this could be very time-consuming. Ask around to see if one is available. If family and friends can't help, libraries, careers offices and local employment projects are worth investigating.

COVERING LETTERS WITH CVS

Covering letters accompanying CVs as part of an on-spec application should deal with the following points:

- make the purpose of the application clear

- be explicit about what position you are looking for

- if no specific job has been advertised and no job description exists, use what general information about the company is available

- pull out key points from the CV

- be explicit about what is being offered to the company, including personal qualities

◆ keep the letter to one side of A4 – and focus on the more important points.

The letter may seem merely to repeat what is contained in the CV. Teachers and trainers know the value of telling people what you're going to talk about (priming them), going ahead and giving the talk, then telling them what you've just talked about (summarising). A similar concept applies to sending in speculative CVs. The covering letter should say what will be found in the CV; the CV lets employers find out for themselves what you've just told them. It provides a lead-in and gives you the opportunity to make sure they don't miss the best of what you have to offer them.

AN ALTERNATIVE CV

A CV that details employment history chronologically is probably the one most commonly used and best expresses the progress in a career, assuming it has been smooth and without a hitch. However, for many people this is not the case, and a chronologically organised CV will serve only to draw attention to gaps and changes.

Don't worry. There is an alternative.

Rather than listing work experience by employer, organise it in terms of the kind of work experience gained in various jobs. Prioritise the experience and skills that will be most appreciated by the prospective employer. The CV on p. 86 might suit an application for a financial manager's post in a company that has some overseas business. The CV's focus is firmly on skills and not on continuity of employment.

If you wish, you can include another heading, WORK EXPERIENCE, simply listing employers and positions held. EDUCATION can also be included if appropriate.

Your covering letter will be the same as for a chronological CV: if it's an 'on-spec' approach, you'll be pulling out key points from the CV and highlighting them in the letter; if for an advertised vacancy the covering letter need only be brief (see Chapter 5).

The benefit of the functional CV is that it draws attention to skills and experience relevant to the job application. An

Max Goodworker
12 Jobly Lane
Workington, CA55 9UP
0100 000000

PROJECT MANAGEMENT

- extensive experience in developing and delivering customer care pro-grammes, mainly in the retail sector
- successfully introduced multi-media training materials to a number of blue-chip clients
- worked within budget and to deadline with 98 per cent of projects

FINANCIAL SKILLS

- introduced PJ100 computerised project-management system, improv-ing successful project completion by an average of 20 per cent
- wide experience of set costing and budgeting procedures
- experience of negotiating and buying services with foreign currencies and successfully integrating variable exchange rates into budget allowances.

INTERNATIONAL

- experience of all major European countries
- proficient written and spoken business languages: Spanish, French, German
- excellent contacts and good working relationships with relevant service providers across Europe, especially Germany, France and Italy

Other Information

- Member of International Project Management Association (IPMA)
- BA Project Management
- Client awarded Best Customer Care (1996) by Retail Association of Europe.

employer's eye can easily be distracted by patchy details of a chronologically arranged CV: different periods of employment, number of employers and varied work environments. They may prove to be far from helpful in affirming your credentials for the new job.

The functional CV also enables you to include non-paying work experience or experience/skills you can bring from unrelated professions or jobs. This is especially useful for anyone who has been out of paid employment or who wishes to make a change of direction in their career. Overall, a functional CV may genuinely offer an employer the fairest chance to assess the applicant's potential and determine their suitability for any vacancy.

Face to Face: The Interview

An interview can resemble a scene around Pop Larkin's kitchen table or Macbeth's meeting with the witches. Interviewers may be as voluble as Mr Bean or as reassuring as Cruella de Vil. Whatever the eventual reality of the experience, the mind tends to dramatise in advance what may be in store.

WHAT INTERVIEWS ARE FOR

Distorted preconceptions about what to expect from an interview, and indeed what they are all about, can badly affect your chances of success. If you approach the interview anticipating a Stalinist interrogation, you're unlikely to go into it with a positive frame of mind. Instead the expectation of a conflict, requiring a victor and a victim, leads invariably to defensiveness and tension. It is not a recipe for warmth and conversational give-and-take.

Interviews are not, generally, interrogations. They are nothing more than exchanges with a shared purpose: to get to know the other person a bit better and find out what they have to offer.

For the employer the interview is to distinguish between a handful of people who look, on paper, to offer more or less what they're looking for – similar skills, qualifications and levels of experience. The employer aims, in the course of the interview, to personalise the CV, to amplify some of the information and to allow the applicant to characterise himself. For the applicant it is an opportunity to talk in more detail about skills and experience, to demonstrate an ability to back up the points highlighted in the application and to generally reassure the employer that you are a personable and genial individual whom it will be a pleasure to employ.

Like any good host, the interviewer will assume responsibility for leading the conversation. There's nothing ominous in this. Although they will take the lead, this should not detract from the aim of the interview, which is for both parties to find that all-important common ground, to discover whether it would be *mutually* profitable for you to fill the post available. Some interviews are more formal than others, some more gruelling (see 'Stress interviews', p. 93), but ultimately all share this goal. If a candidate collapses under the type of heavy questioning which simulates what might reasonably be encountered in the job itself, it is a blessing for candidate and employer alike to find out beforehand. Whatever transpires at interview provides both parties with material on which to base an assessment of your suitability for the job, the job's suitability for your skills and experience, and their suitability as employers.

It is important to retain a sense of the interview as a two-way process. The interviewee is not present merely as a passive respondent to aggressive questions. They have a right to assess the company through the interview process and to ask questions about it when an opportunity presents itself. Often interviewers will deliberately create such an opportunity because the interviewee's questions are revealing. They show the depth of forethought that has gone into preparation for the interview as well as indicating what concerns the interviewee most. And, as an interviewee, it is important to use the interview to add to your knowledge of the company and the job. Is it the same as you imagined it would be when you applied? And, if not, would it be more or less suitable?

PREPARATION

If the key to successful property development rests on three things, location, location, location, then the key to successful interviews probably rests on these three: preparation, preparation, preparation.

To help you prepare, consider the resources you have at your disposal:

- the job advertisement

- the job description and person specification.

- any other information supplied by the company

- a copy of the application form/CV and covering letter

- your network of contacts – use it to find out as much as possible about the company and the person who will be the interviewer

- time.

The person who will be interviewing you will also have:

- your application form/CV and covering letter

- knowledge about the job you're applying for

- job description and person specification

- knowledge about the company.

The main difference between interviewer and interviewee is the depth of knowledge the interviewer has about the job and the company, and the depth of knowledge the interviewee has about him- or herself. This is the basis of the exchange.

The interviewer will use the application form and CV to guide questions during the interview, so it's vitally important for the interviewee to be familiar with what was included. The interviewer will want to ask about the achievements mentioned in the covering letter or CV and will want to see if examples can be given to show instances of when all those personal qualities have come into play. If you have claimed to possess good organisational skills, they'll want to hear how these have been applied and to what effect in the past. If you said you increased turnover in your department or previous job, they'll be eager to hear exactly how you managed it.

Go through the application carefully, along with any other information about the job, and pick out those elements that are likely to prove central to the interview. Try to put yourself in the mind of the interviewer. What are their priorities? What do they most want to establish?

Your network of contacts should also form part of the interview preparation. Through it find out as much up-to-date information as possible – things may have changed since the original application or even since an earlier visit. Also look into what may be encountered at interview, including:

◆ the person or group of people who will be conducting the interview

◆ how their interviews are normally conducted

◆ any tests or assessments that may form part of the interview.

TYPES OF INTERVIEW

Not all employers advise short-listed applicants about who or what to expect at interview, yet what transpires can vary enormously from one employer to another, even for similar vacancies. There is no guarantee that because it was a one-to-one interview with one employer, there will be the same arrangement with the next. Larger employers, especially during mass-recruitment programmes, are more likely to advise applicants of what to expect, including the likely duration of the interview, the number and status of people interviewing candidates, the format of the programme, if it is to be lengthy and any work sampling or tests which will be included. For psychological preparation this information is very helpful. In the absence of such information, either direct or through your network, it will be useful at least to be aware of what may greet you.

ONE-TO-ONE INTERVIEWS

As the name implies, this is where one representative from the company (who may turn out to be the boss, a line manager or someone from Personnel) conducts the interview.

A possible downside to one-to-one interviews is that they tend to be less well structured, sometimes providing few real opportunities for applicants to demonstrate their suitability for the job. The relatively informal approach makes it easier to fall foul of the interviewer's own personal preferences and biases, which may have little to do with whether a candidate could do the job or not. Having said that, if the company is small and you would be expected to work closely with the person conducting the interview, the subjective interpretation of whether a good working relationship could be developed will be important – to both of you.

Throughout one-to-one interviews make sure that the important points are covered about your suitability for the post.

PANEL INTERVIEWS

When more than one person takes part in the interview it is described as a panel interview. Up to six people may comprise the panel. Typically each person represents a specific aspect of the company, so there may be someone from Personnel, the person who would line-manage the post and someone with overall responsibility for the department or section in which the vacancy has arisen. Depending on the type of job, there may be others present, such as someone with specialist knowledge or a representative of an associated body or group (for example, a parent/governor for school appointments).

Although apparently more daunting at first, panel interviews can be easier to handle than one-to-one. With several people involved, preparation tends to be thorough. This means interviewees have a better opportunity to demonstrate their suitability for the job because questions are more structured and focus on eliciting relevant information. This professional, as opposed to informal, approach works in the interviewee's favour, so keep this uppermost in your mind if the prospect of being questioned by a whole team of interviewers is too alarming for words.

Since each panel member has a particular interest in the appointment, they will take it in turn to ask questions about their area of interest. The proceedings will be conducted by the chairperson who will introduce each member, make sure the interview keeps on course and to schedule, and who will open and close the session. All members will probably take notes throughout. It can be off-putting to see someone suddenly start scribbling, but with a number of candidates to interview, note-taking is unavoidable, so try to ignore it.

Panel interviews can be much fairer, being less prone to the problems of personal bias inherent in one-to-one interviews. A panel interview is like a series of micro one-to-one interviews. As proceedings get under way, concentrate on the person asking the questions – give them your full attention – and forget about the others until it is their turn to take the floor.

STRESS INTERVIEWS

All interviews tend to be stressful. This is normal. But some interviews are purposefully conducted to put interviewees under extra pressure. This is not to satisfy some sadistic whim of the interviewer but is a carefully devised strategy employed to see how candidates cope under stress. Applicants for higher management positions or tough, front-line jobs may encounter this technique. For all intents and purposes it amounts to a simulation exercise. How well you perform will be taken as an indication of likely future performance.

Interviewers use different ploys, including bullying, being confrontational, questioning aggressively, interrupting, taking a contrary stance, making personal comments and generally doing whatever they can to try to rattle the candidate. Obviously they won't tell you beforehand that this is what they intend to do, so be alert to the technique. Their aim is to ruffle feathers; yours is to stay unruffled. This is easier said than done but remain centred, remember it is a game and avoid the trap of taking comments personally. Whatever they say, whatever attitude they strike, they are not attacking you but are trying to assess how you react and handle yourself in difficult situations. So stay cool and take it all in a good humour.

ASSESSMENT CENTRES

Assessment centres refer not to places but to multi-part selection procedures. Being anything from half a day to two days in duration, depending on the job and individual employers, they can include combinations of any of the following:

- a one-to-one interview

- a panel interview

- group exercises – to assess interpersonal and team-working skills

- work sampling – to assess how well candidates would be able to perform the job

- written tests – psychometric testing which assesses a person's job-related abilities and aptitudes, their personality and/or personal values. An employer may want to test only one of these

- role-play exercises – to see how candidates would handle themselves in a situation which they may encounter in the job

- presentation exercises – to see how well information can be conveyed to a group of people; used when this would be an important part of the job.

Highly structured interview procedures like these enable employers to get a fuller picture of candidates than is possible through a half-hour interview. From the candidate's point of view it not only removes the pressure of having to give the performance of a lifetime in just thirty minutes or so but also offers an opportunity to shine in a wider range of situations.

TELEPHONE INTERVIEWS

Now being used by some major employers at the initial screening stage, telephone interviews are becoming more prevalent. If you are not prepared for one, it would be easy to blow your chances. If you have been notified that you will be contacted by phone to discuss your application further, this signals a screening interview by phone.

Make sure you're not caught out; have at the ready by the phone your application and personal details, plus pen and paper. Practise your telephone greeting and voice (see below) – how to speak as well as what you say will form an important part of the overall impression a recruiter forms. Interviewers will want to check on relevant abilities and experience – as well as motivation to do the job. Prepare yourself to be asked questions about why you want the job, what experience you can bring to it and situations in the past which demonstrate specific job-related skills.

COMMUNICATING WELL

Although an interview is an exchange of information, the responsibility for making the experience interesting and distinct lies with the interviewee. The interviewer will have a set list of questions for every candidate which won't be adjusted to suit individual applicants very much. So it is up to the interviewee to inject some vitality and originality into what can become a rather stale process. The candidate must pick up cues from the interviewer's questions and use them as interestingly as possible.

LISTENING

It is important to listen closely to the questioner in order to be able to give the most appropriate information as a response. Practise listening skills: hear people out fully before making any conversational responses. Be attentive to the tone of the questions, to any nuances they contain – they may provide the more inviting areas on which to base a reply.

Listening to someone attentively, at a basic level, is an act of good manners. It's a simple way to show interest in them (even interviewers like to be liked) and therefore interest in the company and the job.

SPEAKING

The only way to discover how you come across when you're being asked direct questions is by listening to yourself. Once the initial shock of the unrecognisable sound has passed, analyse precisely how you come across:

- do you speak too loudly or in an inaudible mousy squeak?

- do you tend to over-talk, gabbling on when a single sentence reply would suffice?

- is the pitch of your voice varied enough to make what you have to say sound interesting?

- do you speak clearly? Is it easy to make out what you say?

- is your talk overloaded with ums and ahs?

- do all your answers begin in the same way; with the same word 'Well, ... '?

Listen to recordings objectively – ask family and friends for their opinions too – and practise improving the way you convey information to listeners.

BODY LANGUAGE

Pre-interview nervousness is to be expected – it may be distinctly useful, adding an edge of excitement that will invigorate the interview. It is not helpful if it leaves the interviewee looking cowed and terror-stricken. Craven posture is not going to inspire confidence.

A few simple pointers:

- keep your arms unfolded; folding them across your chest is an unwelcoming, defensive gesture

◆ practise sitting so that you look neither too stiff nor so relaxed that you seem unconcerned or uninterested. A relaxed, upright position, with your legs comfortably placed (not stretched out in front of you), is best. Keep your feet firmly on the ground and sit back in the chair, so that it supports your body comfortably and allows you to move freely, animatedly, as the circumstances require

◆ smile when you greet your interviewer, but a continuous, unwavering Cheshire Cat grin is disconcerting and unnatural

◆ don't hurry. Take your time to settle yourself so that once the interview begins you are quite unselfconscious about posture. This way the interviewer will not be distracted and both interviewer and interviewee can concentrate on what needs to be said.

PRESENTATION

Interviewers are like the rest of the world: for them first impressions do make a difference. In a brief encounter such as an interview, presentation can do much to set the tone at the outset. Presentation is more than the clothes you wear; it is also how you wear them and how you use them to reflect your attitude and personality. The entire image has to be coherent to be effective – old shoes or a crumpled shirt can take the shine off the sharpest of suits. The priorities of successful presentation are:

◆ neatness and cleanliness

◆ appropriateness of clothes. Interviews are not fashion parades or funerals. The appropriate clothes to wear are those that will not look out of place in the work environment and will not draw attention to themselves so that the interviewer remembers little of the conversation because of the glare of the Hawaiian shirt or the musical tinkling of jewellery

- gleaming top and tails – that is, your hair and your shoes: both need to have received a brush-up

- absence of clutter – carrier bags, newspapers, envelopes, umbrellas and other extraneous matter should all be left at home if at all possible. Leave umbrellas outside the interview room at least. Clutter is distracting and suggests disorganisation

- body language (see above)

- personal hygiene.

THE QUESTIONS

It is hard not to think of an interview as a test, but be reassured: you not only have the answers to this specialist subject, you *are* the answer. Many questions will be designed simply to allow interviewees to express themselves.

Your preparation should have given you a good idea of the sorts of question the recruiter will be wanting to ask you and the ground they will want to cover relating to:

- your suitability to meet the demands of the job

- what you've already told them about your skills, abilities, achievements, experience and personal qualities in your application.

In answer to some of the more basic questions you may find yourself repeating what you have already told them in your application. Such questions are often used as warm-up exercises, to relax interviewee and interviewer alike and to begin the conversation.

More searching questions will attempt to reveal the depth of your knowledge and experience. For example, if the job advertisement required good organisational skills, and you claimed to have them in your application, the interviewer will want to ask you in some detail for evidence from previous employment. They may create a hypothetical situation and ask how you would deal with it, expecting your response to reflect good organisation skills.

General questions often crop up at interview. Sounding deceptively simple, they need to be handled effectively. Expect to be asked:

- why do you want this job?

- what can you bring to this job/company?

- tell me about yourself

- why should I offer you the job?

- do you have any questions to ask us?

These seemingly innocuous questions can throw you off balance.

Q. Why do you want this job?

A. Don't indulge in mindless flattery or hint that your interest is purely mercenary. The question is an opportunity to expound your professional motivations, your perceptions of the job, how you see yourself in relation to it, your enthusiasm for it and how it fits with your ambition for your career.

Q. What can you bring to this job/company?

A. Apart from the skills and experience that they already know about, the question provides an opportunity to describe the contribution you would like to make. Mention here any personal qualities you possess, such as keenness for the work, aspects of commitment to the company's aims or an appreciation of the company's client group.

Q. Tell me about yourself.

A. This is such an open question it leaves many an interviewee struggling to know how to begin to answer it. Be prepared. What it is enquiring into is your professional self primarily, though in talking about your working experience the question gives room for more personal details – how your work suits your character, how your hobbies, enthusiasms and academic strengths led you to this kind of work.

Q. Why should I offer you the job?

A. The answer to this question should reassure the interviewer that they would be making the right decision in offering you the job and confirm your ability to match all the key requirements they have set out (or, if no selection criteria have been made available, your anticipation of those requirements).

Q. Do you have any questions to ask us?

A. From your research and preparation, identify any areas that need clarification. Focus on one or two and direct your questions to issues that would fundamentally affect your decision to accept the job. It shows forethought if you have made a written note in advance of any questions and you shouldn't hesitate to consult your notebook at this point (but make sure you're able to turn directly to the page you've written them down on). Often, indeed ideally, the interviewee's questions will have been answered as a result of the ground covered in the interview, in which case just acknowledge the fact when asked. This is particularly true if the employer has given an introductory description of the job and the company. Such remarks should be carefully noted, though, in case they provoke questions in themselves.

Don't expect the interviewer to ignore gaps or anomalies in your CV. Anticipate what they're likely to home in on, and be ready with your answers. A succinct, matter-of-fact approach is normally best. You don't need to say more than is necessary to resolve any doubts they may have.

THE RESULT

If all goes well, the interview should conclude with enthusiasm for the job on the part of the interviewee and a satisfied interviewer. The interview will often wind up with details of when a decision will be reached, and how it will be communicated. Smaller companies may save on the paperwork and articulate the decision there and then, especially if the initial approach was on spec.

JOB OFFERS

If the job is offered to you, acceptance may not necessarily be a straightforward decision. It is most unusual to be asked to decide immediately; the employer will generally allow a couple of days for a candidate's consideration of the various aspects of the offer, some of which will be indirectly connected to the job:

- the work environment and facilities

- aspects to the job, only revealed at interview

- salary

- travel to and from work

- the personalities of co-workers

- different emphases on aspects of the job from the ones you had expected

- fringe benefits

- other job offers in the pipeline

- opportunities for training and development.

It's easy to feel pressured into accepting a job for the wrong reasons – it's almost always helpful to discuss the decision with

friends and family. Just talking about concerns and reserva-
tions often helps put them into a new perspective.

If grave doubts persist and lead to the offer being declined,
turn it down with good grace, in writing, giving whatever
explanation is appropriate while thanking the company for its
interest in your application.

NOT THIS TIME

It can be terribly disappointing not to be offered a job. If this
happens, allow yourself the time and opportunity to acknowledge and come to terms with your disappointment – it will
help if you have other irons in the fire, and a jobhunt routine to
fill the next few days until disappointment passes.

Failure to secure the job may not be personal, but it is
difficult not to look for reasons. Check constructively to see if
there are aspects that can be improved. With the benefit of a
few days' hindsight, assess the interview. If certain questions
caused problems, practise modifying some of the answers for
next time. Use a video camera to record your interview
techniques; play back the tape and examine how you come
across. Professional input can be found at the local Jobcentre
or TEC (address in your phone book) where there are often
courses on interview techniques.

Rejection isn't pleasant, but it comes with the jobhunting
territory. Only one person can be appointed to each post, and
often it can be a marginal impulse that sways the decision. The
more interviews you attend, the more adept you will become
until, when the right job comes along, you'll find yourself
sailing through.

Who's Typical Anyway?

The ideal applicant for a job is young enough to be quick at learning new skills, old enough to offer sound experience, has an unbroken career record, presents no problems with fitting in and is generally the Perfect Employee.

The reality is that many don't conform to this ideal. Recruiters advertise that they're looking for certain skills, abilities and experience but may be hoping for the unobtainable.

For the jobseeker, the thought of having to compete with perfection can seem daunting. But employers are waking up to the fact they can no longer afford to have unrealistic expectations about applicants. As Marks and Spencer's national recruitment manager, Kate Orebi Gann, remarked, 'Few employers have so many suitable applicants that they can afford to disregard a whole sector of the population, whatever their background.'

At last employers are realising that the person they should select to fill a vacancy is the one with the most relevant skills, experience and other qualities required to do the job successfully. All else is about as important as what they have in their sandwiches at lunchtime. As the Institute of Personnel and Development says with reference to equal opportunities in their *Guide on Recruitment*, 'The entire selection process must be based only on criteria related to the requirements of the job, the necessary competences to perform the job and the potential for development.'

Less enlightened attitudes persist, but not in well-run companies. Confronted by them, it's best to leave them be. It's not worth hammering away at their vacancy and insisting to be let in to what might turn out to be less a job opportunity than a sentence for hard labour.

Instead research via your network, and concentrate on those employers who have a reputation for knowing a good thing when it comes along. This is a two-way process. Just as employers are looking for the right person, so you are looking for the right employer.

NO EXPERIENCE

Employers like experienced applicants. The experience is reassuring, answering specific doubts about ability in the job and general concerns about attitude and approach. Lack of experience – because of youth or a decision to make an abrupt career change – will provoke some doubts in employers' minds.

For first jobbers, the problem may not be so great: many jobs are often advertised as suitable for school-leavers or new graduates. Employers also accept that a person who has just left full-time education will have limited experience, if any. Don't try to explain it away. However, you need to beat off the competition from all the other first jobbers applying for the post. And if the approach is unsolicited, the employer will need to be interested by accomplishments other than a list of A-level passes.

Don't dismiss skills and experience that, while not directly connected to the target job, might none the less be useful if adapted. Employers look out for:

- general work experience – which demonstrates aware-ness of what's normally required of any employee, including experience gained through holiday or week-end jobs

- relevant subject knowledge – if you're interested in working in the financial sector, maths and perhaps economics exam passes will be worth mentioning

- non-paid experience – involvement with voluntary or leisure groups can be used to demonstrate your awareness of relevant issues (perhaps social issues, if you're applying for jobs in this field, or more general work-related issues, like an awareness of the importance of team-working skills)

♦ specific skills – again, these may include those acquired outside an education or a training programme but which are transferable to the work place. Familiarity with computers and keyboard skills are definitely worth mentioning

♦ all employers want to hire people who are reliable, good time-keepers, conscientious and keen. Qualities like these can be demonstrated without having to have an impressive record of work experience. For example, good time-keeping is something which would be on school or college reports or integral to the pursuit of leisure activities such as sports-training routines or orchestral participation.

Use the covering letter to spell out for the recruiter those interests which relate most closely to the job and to highlight the personal qualities you can bring to it. If you have a National Record of Achievement, a document containing records of academic and personal achievements which some schools opt to use, you may want to use it to remind you of relevant key points to mention in support of your application. This is also a useful document for school leavers to take along to interview.

Similar points apply to career changers. Consider using the functional CV which concentrates on relevant skills rather than on the environment in which they were acquired. The covering letter should reinforce this, emphasising the transfer-ability of skills, flexibility of attitude and those personal qualities which identify for the employer a good worker with enthusiasm and potential.

A CRIMINAL RECORD

One in three men have a criminal record by the time they're thirty.

Although there are additional considerations for anyone with a record, the same basic principle applies: demonstrate in the CV and covering letter suitability for the job by highlighting relevant skills, experience, abilities and personal qualities.

There is no obligation to declare a criminal record unless directly asked on an application form or in person at interview. If a conviction has become 'spent' – when, effectively, the slate is wiped clean – there is no obligation to declare it even under direct questioning. However, some jobs and professions are excepted from the Rehabilitation of Offenders Act and require all convictions, regardless of whether they have become spent or not, to be declared (see below).

The period of time it takes before convictions become officially spent varies according to the type of crime, age when the crime was committed and length of sentence. Prison sentences of more than two and a half years never become spent. For advice about the period of time relating to your own case, check with a probation officer or contact the Apex Trust or NACRO (see Appendix B).

It is not necessary to mention a criminal record in a CV; if an application form specifically asks for details about convictions, simply put 'see letter' on the application form and include the details on a separate sheet. Mark the envelope 'Private and Confidential', and address it to the employer or personnel manager. This should ensure a greater degree of confidentiality.

NACRO suggests that time spent in prison can be accounted for on application forms and CVs as 'not in employment' or 'change in personal circumstances'. But be prepared to answer questions about this at interview.

Disclosure needs careful consideration. How, when and whether to reveal a criminal record is not straightforward. Discussion with someone from the nearest branch of the Apex Trust and the NACRO leaflet on this issue called 'Disclosing Convictions' may help you decide what to do in your own situation and how best to handle disclosure if you choose to do so voluntarily.

Some careers are effectively closed to people with certain types of criminal record. These include jobs in education, including school caretakers; social work; health, including chemists and dentists; accountancy; the legal professions; even traffic wardens. Jobs within companies which handle defence contracts are also excepted, as are some Civil Service posts. For a more comprehensive list, see the NACRO leaflet 'Rehabilitation of Offenders Act 1974'.

Unless employers claim a vacancy is excepted from the Act, it is open to anyone wishing to apply who believes they are suitable and able to do the job. Your challenge is to catalogue your existing skills and present them to an employer in such a way that your application receives as serious consideration as all others.

If time spent in prison creates a wide gap in your employment history, consider drawing up a functional CV. Highlight some of the following skills and personal qualities which an employer would see as being relevant to the job:

- current driving licence, first-aid certificate, etc.

- relevant training courses, even if they were taken in prison and even if they did not lead to a qualification

- practical and workplace skills you gained while in prison – it is not necessary to say where the skills were gained in a functional CV. Also consider Accreditation of Prior Learning (APL), which enables existing skills and learning to be credited towards a National Vocational Qualification. Contact NACRO for further details (see Appendix B)

- practical skills, such as wood-working or keyboarding

- personal qualities, such as commitment, good communication skills or an ability to work well in a team.

Additional help in finding a job is available through the

Apex Trust, which offers advice, training and support specifically to ex-offenders who are trying to find their way into work. NACRO also runs Jobclubs for ex-offenders and has launched a New Careers Training initiative, which includes training courses, vocational guidance and jobsearch skills.

THE 'WRONG' SEX

Thanks to the Sex Discrimination Act 1975, it is now illegal to discriminate against someone because they are perceived by an employer to be the 'wrong' sex for the job. A man wanting to work in the nursing profession or as a secretary should find nothing more to stop him from applying than a woman wanting to be a steeplejack or firefighter. With the relevant skills, qualifications and experience required to do the job an application should be judged on these merits alone. The only exceptions to this are jobs in which being a particular sex is what the Act refers to as being a 'genuine occupational qualification'. If this is the case, it should be made clear in the advertisement along with reference to the Sex Discrimination Act.

It is very difficult to prove sexual discrimination – and even a successful court case will not lead to a job. No company can be compelled to employ a person; they will be fined and you may receive some compensation. But it is important that incidents of discrimination are registered so that the perpetrators are known and the practice eliminated.

RETURNING TO WORK

If you've spent time away from paid employment, whether for child-rearing, caring for a sick relative, backpacking to beyond or writing that novel, a priority will be to convince yourself that you can handle a return to work. It's easy to lose confidence about being able to manage, and keep up with, the demands of a job.

Reassurance helps: if you've raised a family, run a home and kept up some sort of social life, then you're bound to be able to cope with being employed. The demands will be different, and it may take a while to settle down into a new routine and work environment, but that goes for any newcomer to an organisation.

Instead of going straight into jobhunting, address the matter of lost ground to be made up. Become familiar with developments which may have taken place during your absence. Read up in the trade press about current topics, trends and progress. Make contact with former work colleagues and gradually start to mingle in professional circles again. Attend conferences, investigate courses to update rusty skills or develop new ones and begin the process of reintegration into the world of work. This won't only boost confidence; it will provide employers with evidence that you still have your finger on the professional pulse. Some of your preparation will help at the application stage, the rest at interview.

Re-entering the nine-to-five routine can be quite a shock to the system and lead to further stress if you're not prepared for it. Toe-dipping may help. Consider temporary or voluntary work – even work experience with friends or family – to give you confidence in your abilities. This will come through at interview and serve to reassure prospective employers about your proficiency.

A functional CV would probably be a more effective self-advertisement than a chronological one, which would emphasise the breaks in career or work pattern. The CV should provide an opportunity to draw together skills gained outside the work environment:

- time-management skills

- budget control

- organisational skills

- experience of different cultures

- communication or keyboard skills

- skills developed as a result of involvement in school or other voluntary activities, like fund-raising or chairing meetings

- flexibility

- adaptability

- interpersonal skills

- ability to manage change.

Make a job application a forum for demonstrating that you have not only the necessary qualifications for the job but additional skills which would be difficult to find in anyone without your unique life experiences. A period of time spent out of employment need not count against you.

PAST IT?

In the USA it's against the law to discriminate against someone's job application because of age. You won't find references to age in their job advertisements. In the UK we still have a long way to go. Although there is official opposition to age discrimination, there is, at the moment, no legislation to back it up. The Employers Forum on Age claims that age most commonly counts against applicants after they reach fifty.

The Campaign for Older Workers aims to encourage the voluntary removal of age barriers to jobs. Many employers with foresight, such as the Littlewoods Organisation plc and Sainsbury's, have recruitment policies which reflect their awareness of the benefits of employing people outside the thirty- to forty-year-old age barrier. More mature workers tend to bring better attitudes to work, stay committed to their jobs, can often handle customers better and, obviously, bring much more experience to bear on the work they do.

With changing demographics, older workers may well start to come into their own. Many employment agencies are realising this. For example, Manpower plc helps people wanting to develop their career or make career changes and provides free training or retraining – reportedly with great success with people from the age of forty-five upwards.

As with any contender for a job, older applicants need to make sure their skills are relevant and up to date, and that the

CV and covering letter highlight the abilities and qualities an employer is looking for. The letter and CV should demonstrate improvements, increased profits, reduced staff turnover or whatever other advantages previous employers have gained rather than limply and vaguely talking about 'many years of experience'. Be specific and don't be modest about your achievements.

Play to your strengths. With wider experience you may find it easier than most to make use of contacts in both your professional and personal life to help you network your way into work. Your communication skills will be much better than those of a twenty-year-old and your presence more assured. Capitalise on these.

DISABILITIES

There appears to be a long way to go before employers stop making ill-considered decisions that militate against jobfinders on the grounds of disability. They are slow to realise that the right person for a job is the one who can bring the relevant skills, experience and personal qualities, not whether they happen to bring a walking stick or guide-dog to work as well.

However, with the introduction of the Disability Discrimination Act in 1996, things are starting to move in the right direction. The Act states that it is now unlawful for employers with twenty employees or more to treat a person differently because of a disability unless there is a good reason for doing so. This means that smaller businesses are exempt from this ruling and that larger employers are still able to discriminate if they believe they are justified in doing so. Although the Act helps, obviously there is room for improvement.

In the meantime, when making a job application prior research into the employer, the work environment and how the work is carried out at present is advisable. It will provide an idea of the sorts of obstacle an employer is likely to have uppermost in their mind when considering a disabled applicant for the job. Although you may not want to mention your disability at the application stage, be prepared for the concerns that may be voiced at interview.

The 'Positive About Disabled People' symbol is now used by over 3,000 employers and should help to raise the awareness of other employers about the need to treat applicants with disabilities fairly and to give their applications equal consideration. Channel Four, the Body Shop, BUPA and Royal Mail, as well as many local councils and smaller employers, use the symbol.

Employers who adopt the symbol guarantee to interview applicants with disabilities as long as they meet the minimum criteria for the job. This doesn't mean a job offer will automatically follow; the interview stage is competitive and a disabled applicant will still have to demonstrate they are the person most suitably qualified. But the symbol ensures that a disabled candidate will not be filtered out at the first stage for the wrong reasons.

If a company displays the symbol, it may benefit your application to mention your disability. This is also the case with employers who, while not part of the 'Positive About Disabled People' scheme, make an equal-opportunities statement in job advertisements and recruitment literature.

Use your network to research employers you would like to work for. Also contact the local library to find out if there are any local groups which offer advice or other employment-related support to people with disabilities. If there is a national organisation concerned with your disability, you may want to contact it to find out what help or guidance it can provide.

Jobcentres have disability employment advisers whom you should contact for additional help in jobfinding. They often have links with the local employers who have good recruitment practices. They will discuss with an employer the need for any special equipment or adaptations to the work environment.

Awareness of the potential of workers with disabilities, especially in electronic technologies, is gradually reaching more enlightened employers. The high profile of people like Stephen Hawking, David Blunkett MP, and Spike Milligan, who is renowned for his lifelong battle with depressive illness, helps to reinforce the message that having a disability does not prevent someone from being creative, intellectually brilliant or professionally competent. But until it is unlawful for employers, regardless of the size of their business, to discriminate on the grounds of disability it will be more rewarding and effective to target enlightened people and the businesses they run.

ETHNIC MINORITIES

Discriminating against applicants on the grounds of race, colour, ethnic origins or nationality is against the law (Race Relations Act 1976). But this does not prevent some employers from sending out 'We regret to inform you . . . ' letters to applicants from ethnic minority groups. Figures from a survey carried out in 1996 by recruitment specialists Austin Knight showed that 65 per cent of the people they interviewed who were from ethnic minorities complained of having experienced racial discrimination. Census data from 1991 shows that the incidence of unemployment among Caribbean people was two and a half times higher than among their white counterparts.

Although there are some employers who are short-sighted enough to operate in this way, it is not the practice of all employers. Use your network to find out about the better employers in your area.

Make sure your CV and covering letter reflect your suitability for the job and focus on your relevant skills, experience, personal qualities and what you have achieved in previous jobs. If English is not your first language, get someone to check your application before it is submitted. Faced with piles of applications in response to an advertised vacancy, employers look for quick, simple ways to decide who to short-list and who not. Poor spelling and shaky grammar are one reason to reject an application.

Find out if specialist local help is available. The local library should have details of any special projects which might be appropriate; the Jobcentre may also have details of specialist Jobclubs or other schemes operating in the area for which you might be eligible. Having the right sort of support could make all the difference in terms of tailoring the application and acquiring the confidence to succeed.

Evidence of discrimination on the grounds of ethnic background should be reported to the Commission for Racial Equality (see Appendix B).

9

Moving Forward

Jobfinding is an unpredictable business at the best of times. There are so many different factors which affect it, many beyond the control of the jobfinder. Luck, being in the right place, happening to overhear someone mention a new vacancy – these are all considerations which can affect the speed of success. But sooner or later all the disparate elements of the search will come together. It eventually happened for David, a former Consett steelworker, after sixteen years and for Bob, a former regional manager, after hundreds of job applications over an eighteen-month period. But jobfinding doesn't necessarily take so long.

It pays to keep an eye on how you're doing so that you can assess your rate of progress. This is what successful businesses do, and if it works for them, there's no reason why it won't help you succeed too.

YOUR PROGRESS REPORT

Make notes about your jobhunt activities. This isn't simply to occupy the time. Without the raw data it's almost impossible to assess progress objectively. Keeping a log will provide facts, not just selective memories of what has passed. The log should show:

- ◆ the publications you have checked for job advertisements, how often and the outcome

- ◆ the places you have checked, how often and the outcome

- contacts you have made and the outcome

- networking events you have attended and the outcome

- speculative enquiries you have made, how you made them and the outcome of each

- leads you have followed up and the outcome

- job applications made and their progress

- interviews attended, your performance and the outcome.

Looking back over a month's progress enables you to see:

- the areas that might have been neglected

- activities which yield good results

- activities which don't seem to pay off

- leads that have not been followed up

- points in the application procedure in which you may be weak

- the progress you have made and what you have learned from the process up to now.

Analysis might reveal any of the following:

'I'm not finding advertised the jobs I'm looking for.' If this is the case, check:

- you're not overlooking a key trade publication

- how other people got their foot in the door; you may find that a more circuitous route, like temping, is the best way in

- you're networking as well as you can

◆ other geographical areas or opportunities in other countries

◆ the state of your target profession as a whole; it may be in sharp decline

◆ you're making the best of speculative approaches.

'I find the jobs but I'm getting nowhere with my applications.' Check:

◆ the vacancies are suitable, appropriate to your skills and level of experience

◆ the presentation of your application forms; if your handwriting and/or spelling isn't up to much, get some help

◆ the CV and covering letters; make sure they highlight achievements as well as skills and experience

◆ if you're applying only for advertised vacancies, where the competition is always much stiffer, consider 'on spec' approaches and making better use of your network

◆ what employers are currently looking for in your particular field, and whether further training or a skills update would increase your employability.

'I'm getting nowhere at interview.' Check:

◆ interview technique and presentation

◆ responses to questions

◆ ways to help you relax if nerves are getting the better of you

◆ feedback from a recent interview – but be careful not to give the impression that you're challenging their decision not to offer you the job

- whether you were fully prepared

- whether your CV implies more than an employer feels you can deliver

- whether you convey enthusiasm during interviews.

It's only by assessing your progress regularly that you'll find out which areas could do with some special attention. Small changes can often make a significant difference, but if there has been no sign of success after, say, six months, you may want to think about input from elsewhere.

Jobclubs provide jobhunt support and advice, as well as offering free use of facilities like telephones and photocopiers, and access to relevant newspapers and magazines. Support and encouragement, plus a bit of objective assessment and advice, can make all the difference to the outcome of jobfinding activities. Many Jobclubs target specific groups of people, from executives to ex-offenders. Contact the nearest Jobcentre to find out what facilities are available locally. Research available training courses on topics such as interview techniques. The local library or careers centre should have details.

NEW WORK OPTIONS

The majority of people looking for work would prefer full-time, regular employment – a 'normal' job. But opportunities for non-traditional patterns of work are now increasingly arising.

PORTFOLIO WORKING

The biggest growth sector in recent years has been part-time work. Once seen predominantly as the preserve of women who used it to dovetail with child-care and home-making responsibilities, part-time work has taken on a new importance. Now you'll find men and women, professionals and unskilled workers alike, taking advantage of its flexibility.

Unless it's as the chair of a privatised utility or a quango, one part-time job of a few hours a week isn't usually going to pay the bills, but new thinking has brought to the fore the concept of having a collection, or portfolio, of part-time jobs. Even the government has started to support the portfolio approach and provides a financial incentive to encourage unemployed people to take up part-time posts. Ask your client adviser at the Jobcentre about current benefit entitlements. Their aim is to make it financially more feasible for people to take up part-time work.

Having more than one part-time job will save money on National Insurance (NI) payments. As contributions are linked to income received from individual jobs (rather than to the combined total of income received from all jobs) for each and every job, money earned below the lower earnings limit will be free of NI contributions.

Tax can be a little more problematic. Personal allowances are set against the income from whichever is considered to be a person's main job. Income from other jobs will attract the basic rate of tax. This is pretty straightforward unless the income from no individual job is high enough to accommodate the full amount of personal allowances. If this is the case for you, contact the local Inland Revenue office (addresses in telephone directories) for advice on how best to arrange tax payments. A visit in person is probably better than trying to sort things out over the phone. Take along details of present tax allowances, work situation and income. Temp workers will be provided with a form, P625, which enables people to keep account of work done, thus helping to simplify their tax affairs.

Portfolio working requires more vigilance on the tax front than full-time jobs. If the Inland Revenue or your employers get things wrong, it may take until the end of the tax year before any over-payments are refunded, so it is worth spending time on making sure your affairs are organised properly at the outset.

Apart from these minor difficulties, the benefits of portfolio working include:

♦ greater security – if one job is lost through redundancy or market change, there is still at least one other source of income

- gaining a wide range of experience in several working environments

- a wider range of opportunities and contacts, offering more networking opportunities

- part-time work is a growing area – you may find it easier to find two or more part-time vacancies than one full-time position

- its usefulness as a route into full-time employment in one job, if this remains your aim.

Company directors, MPs and even vicars can now be found working with a portfolio of jobs, like the Revd Robert Marshall, who works part-time at a church in London, is a freelance Christian communications consultant, acts as press secretary for the Archbishop of York and is Adviser to the Anglican Diocese in Europe. Beating this is Max Comfort, who not only runs the London Ecohouse project but also has six other part-time jobs. You may want to give this option your serious consideration to improve your chances of employment success.

SHORT-TERM CONTRACT WORK

The belief in a job for life is fast disappearing: it seems unrealistic and is, by some, unwanted. Employers no longer provide long-term guarantees for staff; employees no longer regard their commitment to a company as an obligation for life.

Out of this situation has emerged the culture of short-term contract work. This offers a guarantee of employment for a specific length of time; anything from a few weeks or months to two years. At the end of the agreed period the contract ends.

For some the prospect of short-term contract work holds little appeal, even sheer terror. However, with careful management continuous employment is possible. It is not unusual for contracts to be renewed or extended, and workers in industries such as the media, where short contracts are becoming the norm, become used to networking routinely before the end of each contract. Many jobs, such as that of a camera operator, pay very well, so that if the income is sensibly budgeted, it will cover periods of unemployment.

As with portfolio work, the tax situation may become complex if the contracts are very short. Some contract workers simplify their tax affairs by setting up a private company. Although this involves additional costs in accountancy and registration fees, it streamlines the tax situation and makes it easier to move between one contract and another. For information about whether this would be a good option for you, discuss it with your accountant or tax office. Alternatively, contact the charity Taxaid, which gives free advice on tax problems (see Appendix B).

Short-term contract work may not be many people's preference when they start looking for work, but many find its flexibility stimulating and rewarding.

TELEWORKING

New information technology and the need for employers to cut costs and overheads have led to the development of 'remote working', usually referred to as teleworking.

Essentially this involves working at home while remaining in 'tele' contact with the main office, centre or base, although some 'core' time in the office may be scheduled by the employer for meetings, training and regular face-to-face contact. Teleworking is certainly a growing phenomenon. The company ICL has had homeworkers for the past twenty years, and now BT, the FI Group, Rank Xerox and even the Ministry of Defence have joined the band of employers who are making teleworking positions available which can reduce overheads substantially. For the employee it offers the flexibility of working from home, as if you were self-employed, combined with the support and security which come with being employed. But it does lack the social benefits found in office environments and can cause difficulties if training, advice and support are not regularly supplied.

Use your network to find out about which employers use teleworkers, and make contact with them. In addition, make speculative approaches suggesting teleworking to employers whose business, or some aspects of it, could be run on that basis.

JOBSHARING

Jobsharing is becoming ever more popular. Although it has been around for some time and is therefore not exactly 'new', it will be to many who have focused jobhunt activities on the full-time option.

Jobsharing means that two or more people share the hours, work, responsibilities and benefits of a single full-time post. Although it entails working part-time hours, a jobshare post is not the same as a part-time job, which is normally defined by a self-contained job specification and, importantly, carries fewer in-work benefits. For example, Gary works part-time in the telesales department attached to a local department store. Because of the number of hours he works he is not eligible to join the company's pension scheme. Joan works for the same company, jobsharing the full-time post of marketing manager and working the same number of hours as Gary. However, as the full-time post carries with it eligibility to the company pension scheme Joan is able to benefit.

Salaries and other financial benefits in jobshare posts are split on a pro-rata basis according to the hours each person works. This will be fifty–fifty if the hours are equally divided, sixty–forty if one works three days and the other two. Each person keeps their own entitlement to personal tax allowances.

The benefits of jobsharing include:

♦ many of the bonuses of portfolio working; indeed, a jobshare could form one or more elements of your complete portfolio

♦ jobshares offer better conditions of service than part-time jobs (at least in the UK; the situation differs across Europe)

♦ jobshares can be found at all levels, so career progression won't be jeopardised

- sharing a job with another person facilitates the transfer of new skills

- the flexibility to integrate other lifestyle and/or professional elements into your work pattern; for example, a jobshare could be combined with part-time study or support a career change which initially doesn't pay well.

Jobsharing may mistakenly be presumed to be convenient only for working mothers: in fact it offers opportunities for *everyone*.

SELF-EMPLOYMENT

Frustrated with the lack of opportunities to make use of their skills, experience and enthusiasm, many decide to turn to self-employment – about one person in eight in the UK.

Although it offers a solution to the problem of finding suitable employment, it is not necessarily an easy option. Figures show that the dream of successfully working for yourself fades within the first five years of trading for nine out of ten who try. Grim statistics. But don't let this put you off. Other figures show that 80 per cent of people who become self-employed *stay* self-employed, so it obviously remains an attractive option to the majority.

Lack of business skills and under-investment are often the reasons behind failed enterprises. Minimise the risk by taking full advantage of the professional help available. Government-sponsored business-skills training courses are free or at subsidised rates in some areas. Information on these and the full range of support for new businesses is available through the network of local Business Links. Phone the Business Link Signpost Line on 0345 567765 for details of your nearest branch. They will also advise you of grants for which you may be eligible under the Business Start-Up scheme. Young entrepreneurs should contact the Prince's Youth Business Trust (see Appendix B), which also offers grants.

Having a scintillating idea for a business and throwing vast amounts of money into it are not enough to guarantee success.

Research and planning are vital. Their purpose is to demonstrate that the proposed venture would be viable before sinking a lifetime's savings into it. Information gleaned from research will form the basis of the business plan, a document which is a tool, not just an academic exercise designed to put you through your paces. Banks and other potential backers study business plans rigorously in order to assess applications for loans or other requests for financial help, so you need to have yours thoroughly prepared. Even entrepreneurs who are able to finance business start-ups independently need to draw up plans. Besides providing a way in which to work through, develop and refine the initial idea, the finished plan is a working document in itself. Once a business is up and running, consulting it periodically provides a way in which to check whether everything is on course.

Business Links provide personal business advisers to help people to draw up business plans, and there are many books currently available on the subject, but briefly business plans contain:

- an outline of the business concept

- the unique selling point – that is, what makes the idea different from any other

- the target market – who the customers or clients will be

- market-research results – which should demonstrate clearly that a market exists for the product or service

- marketing plans – how the target market will be reached and how people will find out about the business

- finance, including funding, cashflow projections, pricing (what you will charge), costings (of raw materials and other overheads), capital expenditure

- locations, staffing, premises

- anticipated growth and development plans

- other items relevant to your own specific business, such as health and safety considerations, registration with professional bodies, certification, licences and so on.

It may seem like a lot of work, but if it shows that the idea is not practical, you'll be saving yourself a lot of heartache further down the line. On the other hand, it may simply signal problem areas which need resolving beforehand to avoid difficulties later on.

Self-employment often overlaps with portfolio working – the flexibility of self-employment means it can be combined with other employment interests. Indeed, many people make the transition to full self-employment gradually and, as I did myself, continue to work part-time until the venture starts making a profit. Others combine it with child-care, voluntary work or any number of different income-generating activities. Self-employment allows people to style a working life to suit individual needs, which is the essence of its appeal.

Full of enthusiasm for self-employment but short on ideas? Self-assessment is a good place to start:

- what marketable skills do you have (perhaps ones gained in previous jobs)?

- do you have a natural flair – for example, for throwing parties, catering or dressing with style?

- what knowledge or experience do you have that could form the basis of consultancy work?

- do your hobbies and interests offer any possibilities?

- which previous jobs suggest ideas for self-employment?

Consider too:

- growing sectors of the economy – for example, information technology

- gaps in the market for a service or product

- inventions

- importing and/or exporting

- buying an existing business

- buying into a franchise

- buying and selling

- making, manufacturing or producing items

- the needs of people and businesses in your locality.

CO-OPERATIVES

Bearing the sole responsibility for running a business may seem too daunting a prospect. Working co-operatively in a joint venture with other people may prove to be the answer.

Setting up and running a business as a co-op means that everyone has an equal say, an equal financial input and an equal share of profits. No one has more power than another, and neither does one person gain more financially than another, unless everyone agrees they should.

There are some 45,000 co-ops across the EU, with 9,000 in the UK alone. Practically any business can be set up as a worker co-operative, like The Graphics Company in Edinburgh and Neals Yard Bakery in London. They are often assumed to be small, local ventures, but the successful company Paperback in east London, with a multi-million-pound turnover, proves otherwise. Some co-ops emerge from employee buy-outs of existing companies.

To learn how co-ops work, see if you can visit one in your local area to talk about their experience and what's involved. To investigate further, contact your nearest Co-operative Development Agency or the Industrial Common Ownership Movement (see Appendix B). Both can advise on available grants, loans, training and support.

COMMUNITY BUSINESSES

These ventures are set up in response to the specific needs of communities, which may be for a particular service or in order to generate jobs. Examples include nurseries, retail shops, cafés, business centres, manufacturing, contract cleaning and so on. Profits generated from these ventures are ploughed back into the community itself, either to create more jobs or to fund other local initiatives.

The good thing about community businesses is that they don't require people to sink their own money into them. The corollary to this is that since you don't 'own' a business, you won't benefit personally from profits made, which is a fundamental difference between commercial and community businesses. However, setting up a community business opens the doors to enterprise and employment for many who might otherwise be excluded.

Monies are available from many sources (see Appendices A and B). Check out:

♦ funds administered by your local council

♦ European Social Fund

♦ charitable foundations and trusts

♦ corporate givers and sponsors

♦ National Lottery funds.

While not being 'commercial' in the full sense, community businesses still have to prove themselves viable and be run professionally. No potential backer will hand over funds unless they are convinced the enterprise will succeed, serve identified needs and be managed by people with the professional skills to make it work. Funders monitor progress and financial management carefully and observe the financial disciplines of the most rigorous blue-chip company.

If you like the idea of setting up and running a business but don't have the money to do so; if you can come up with the idea for a business which would serve the identified needs of your community; and if you're not interested in making anything more than a modest salary from the venture, then think about getting together with some like-minded others (if you don't like the idea of going it alone) and consider the community business option.

WORKING ABROAD

The global economy is here and so too are global businesses. European frontiers are disappearing. And from all these changes are emerging new employment opportunities.

If jobs are scarce in your area, consider where else you could make use of your existing skills. Jobcentres are now linked to a Europe-wide database. Ask at your local Jobcentre about current job opportunities in countries throughout the EU for people with your skills. While you're there, check the current regulations about claiming benefit when visiting other EU countries to look for work.

Find out about opportunities abroad through:

◆ foreign newspapers

◆ specialist employment agencies

◆ writing to companies with an international base

◆ contacting foreign embassies, which will often advise, put you into contact with relevant bodies, and give you access to their national newspapers

◆ writing to foreign companies with operations in the UK

◆ networking through contacts, friends and families abroad.

Taking up long-term, even permanent, work abroad needs a lot of careful thought and planning, especially if you have children. Living and working in a country is not the same as holidaying there. If possible, find someone in your network to talk to about their experiences or those of someone they know.

There are plenty of books now available on working abroad; they cover general aspects of the subject as well as specific countries (see Appendix A).

THE VOLUNTARY SECTOR

Involvement in a voluntary group or charity was once the preserve of retired generals and genteel ladies. Now it's big business. Tackling those social problems which local councils are unable to, they now have a wider range of funding sources, including the European Social Fund and the National Lottery.

Emerging in line with these recent developments are paid work opportunities, up to the highest level. Voluntary groups have turned professional in order to survive, and even many smaller groups now have paid staff. Openings exist for development executives, heads of finance, fundraisers, project managers, marketing personnel and trainers, administrative and clerical staff. Larger organisations, like Oxfam, have well-defined career structures and staff-development programmes akin to those of their commercial counterparts. There is now considerable cross-over between the 'commercial' and 'voluntary' sectors.

Although you could make contact with registered charities and voluntary groups which interest you and whose aims you support, they tend not to welcome 'on spec' applications for jobs. However, setting up a meeting to discuss the work they do rather than possible future openings and how they advertise could pay off in the longer term. If immediate vacancies seem unlikely, it may be opportune in the meantime to consider becoming involved as a volunteer.

When vacancies do arise, many smaller organisations advertise in the local press. Specialist magazines and journals are also used, so consult those that relate to the field in which you would like to work. The *Directory of Volunteering and Employment Opportunities*, published by the Directory of Social Change, indicates in which media the organisations it lists normally advertise vacancies.

National newspapers which carry job advertisements in the voluntary sector include the *Guardian* on Wednesdays and the *Independent* on Thursdays. Vacancies can sometimes be found in *The Times* too. Recruitment agencies and Jobcentres are also used to find people to fill lower-grade posts in voluntary groups. For higher-level positions many use specialist agencies, like Charity People, Charity Recruitment and Charity Appointments (see Appendix B).

Working abroad is also an option. Voluntary Service Overseas (VSO) is the organisation which arranges placements throughout Africa, Asia, the Caribbean and the Pacific. While posts attract only local pay rates, the experience often counts for more and appears to work in your favour when applying for jobs once you return. The organisation responds to requests from both government and non-government agencies for a wide range of professionals. Placements have included systems analysts, engineers, business advisers, accountants, publishers and social workers and give some indication of the wide range of skills in demand.

The selection criteria applicants must meet are:

◆ be between twenty-five and sixty years of age

◆ a degree-level education

◆ a professional qualification

◆ at least two years' post-qualification experience

◆ no dependent children

◆ unrestricted right to re-enter the UK

◆ be open to learning about new ways in which to work.

The Volunteer Centre UK is also able to advise on opportunities in Europe (see Appendix B for how to contact it and VSO).

Voluntary work can often lead unexpectedly to paid work opportunities. This may be something to consider integrating into your schedule while you're looking for work. Even if it doesn't lead directly to a job, it helps to keep your CV 'live' and often impresses potential employers that you've found a way to utilise your skills and gain valuable work experience despite being out of work. It also increases opportunities for networking. Contact your local volunteer bureau.

The media constantly offer reminders and reports of how the world of work is changing and becoming more competitive, more aggressive and more demanding. Understandably this can strike fear into the hearts of jobfinders. The jobfinding process is becoming more complex, with less certain outcomes than people even ten years ago could reasonably expect. Employers now want flexibility in their workforce and new skills – even multi-skills. As a result new options are starting to appear which we would be foolish to let drift by without considering how they might work for us, not against us. It is these new opportunities and new pathways that will lead into the world of work.

Appendix A
Further Reading

Applying for jobs

The Perfect CV, Tom Jackson (Piatkus, 1994)
Readymade Job Search Letters, Lynn Williams (Kogan Page, 1995)

Your Readymade CV (CD-Rom) (Kogan Page, 1996)

Communication skills

Confident Conversation: How to Talk in Any Business or Social Situation, Lillian Glass (Piatkus, 1991)

Make That Call, Iain Maitland (Kogan Page, 1996)

Successful Networking, Donna Fisher and Sandy Vilas (Thorsons, 1996)

Your Voice, Andrew Armitage (Right Way, 1992)

Company research

Kelly's business directory. Company information

The Municipal Yearbook and Public Services Directory. Details every organisation in the public sector

The Personnel Manager's Yearbook (AT Information Services, 1996). Contact names and company information

UK Kompass Register. Basic company information

Who Owns Whom (Dun and Bradstreet)

The Guardian Guide to the UK's Top Companies 1995/6, edited by Roger Cowe (Fourth Estate)

Employment rights and advice

'Contracts of Employment', PL801 (REV 3) (DTI; free booklet from Employment Service offices)

'Time Off for Job Hunting or to Arrange Training when Facing Redundancy', PL703 (REV 3) (DTI; free booklet from Employment Service offices)

'Too Old . . . Who Says?' (DfEE; free booklet: tel. 01709 888688)

Your Employment Rights, Michael Malone (Kogan Page, 1992)

'A Brief Guide to the Disability Discrimination Act' (free booklet; tel. 0345 622633; textphone 0345 622644)

The Disabled Person (Employment) Acts 1944, 1958; NI Acts 1945, 1960

Fair Employment (NI) Acts 1976, 1989

Race Relations Act 1976

Rehabilitation of Offenders Act 1974; Exceptions Order 1979

Sex Discrimination Act 1975; Sex Discrimination (NI) Order 1976 and Amendment

Interviews

Great Answers to Tough Interview Questions, Martin Yate (Kogan Page, 1992)

How to Pass Graduate Recruitment Tests, Mike Bryon (Kogan Page, 1994)

How to Pass Selection Tests, Mike Bryon and Sanjay Modha (Kogan Page, 1991)

Your Aptitude Test (CD-Rom) (Kogan Page, 1996)

New work options

Life Without Work, Christine Ingham (Thorsons, 1994)

New Work Options, Christine Ingham (Thorsons, 1996)

How to Get a Job Abroad, Roger Jones (How To Books, 1991)

Overseas Jobs Express (subscription magazine; tel. 0127 345 4522)

Working Abroad, Godfrey Golzen (Kogan Page, 1996)

Community Start Up (National Extension College)

Directory of Grant-Making Trusts (Charities Aid Foundation)

Grants from Europe (NCVO)

Guide to the Major Trusts (Directory of Social Change)

How to Work for a Charity on a Paid or Voluntary Basis, Jan Brownfoot and Frances Wilkes (Directory for Social Change, 1994)

How to Prepare a Business Plan, Edward Blackwell (Kogan Page, 1996)

101 Ways to Start Your Own Business, Christine Ingham (Kogan Page, 1997)

Your Business Start-Up (CD-Rom) (Kogan Page, 1996)

The Indispensable Guide to Working from Home (free BT booklet; tel. 0800 800878)

Job Sharing, Pam Walton (Kogan Page, 1990)

Working Well at Home, Christine Ingham (Thorsons, 1995)

Appendix B
Useful Addresses

Community businesses

Community Development Foundation, 60 Highbury Grove, London N5 2AG; tel.
0171 226 5375. For information on setting up and running a community business

Co-operatives

Industrial Common Ownership Movement, Vassalli House, 20 Central Road, Leeds
LS1 6DE; tel. 0113 246 1737/8. For information on setting up and running a co-
operative business

Disability

Royal Association for Disability and Rehabilitation, 250 City Road, London EC1V
8AS; tel. 0171 250 3222 or minicom 0171 250 4119. Employment help and advice
for people with disabilities

Employment agencies

Age Works; tel. 0171 371 5411. A service for older workers – part of Ecco Employment Agencies

Association of Temporary and Interim Executive Services, c/o FRES, 36–38 Morti-
mer Street, London W1N 7RB; tel. 0171 323 4300. For information on temporary
work for business executives

Charity Appointments; tel. 0171 247 4502. Agency specialising in work with charities

Charity People; tel. 0171 620 0062. As above

Charity Recruitment, tel. 0171 833 0770. As above

Employment Agencies Standards Service; tel. 0645 555105. For difficulties with
employment agencies

Part-Time Careers, 10 Golden Square, London W1R 3AF; tel. 0171 437 3103.
Agency specialising in part-time vacancies

Recruit; tel. 01442 233550. Agency for older workers

Enterprise advice

Business Links; tel. 0345 567765. A government initiative providing a complete
nationwide information service about setting up and running your own business.
For details of the nearest Business Link telephone their Signpost Line, given
above

LiveWIRE, Hawthorn House, Forth Banks, Newcastle-upon-Tyne NE1 3SG; tel.

0191 261 5584. Enterprise support and advice for sixteen- to twenty-five-year-olds, sponsored by Shell UK Ltd

Prince's Youth Business Trust, 5th Floor, 5 Cleveland Place, London SW1Y 6JJ; tel. 0171 321 6500. Support and advice for young entrepreneurs

Equal opportunities

Commission for Racial Equality, Elliot House, 10–12 Allington Street, London SW1E 5EH; tel. 0171 828 7022 or

Hanover House, 45–51 Hanover Street, Edinburgh EH2 2PJ; tel. 0131 226 5186

Equal Opportunities Commission, Overseas House, Quay Street, Manchester M3 3NN; tel. 0161 833 9244 or

Stock Exchange House, 7 Nelson Mandela Place, Glasgow G2 1NQ; tel. 0141 248 5833 or

Caerwys House, Windsor Lane, Cardiff CF1 1LB; tel. 01222 343552

Ex-offenders

APEX Trust, St Alphage House, Wingate Annexe, 2 Fore Street, London EC2Y 5DA; tel. 0171 638 5931. Helps ex-offenders into employment or self-employment

NACRO – National Association for the Care and Resettlement of Offenders, 169 Clapham Road, London SW9 0PU; tel. 0171 582 6500

Financial advice

Taxaid Charitable Trust, 340 Kilburn High Road, London NW6 2QJ; tel. 0171 624 3768. For free information and advice on tax matters

New work options

New Ways to Work, 309 Upper Street, London N1 2TY; tel. 0171 226 4026. For information on all types of flexible working

People with disabilities

Royal Association for Disability and Rehabilitation, 250 City Road, London EC1V 8AS; tel. 0171 250 3222, or minicom 0171 250 4119. Employment help and advice for people with disabilities

Teleworking

National Association of Teleworking; tel. 01761 413869

Telecottage Association; tel. 0800 616008

Volunteering

National Association of Volunteer Bureaux; tel. 0121 327 0265

National Centre for Volunteering in Scotland; tel. 01786 479593

REACH; tel. 0171 928 0452. Part-time voluntary work for professional people

Voluntary Service Overseas, 317 Putney Bridge Road, London SW15 2PN; tel. 0181 780 2266. For voluntary placements abroad

Volunteer Centre UK, Carriage Row, 183 Eversholt Street, London NW1 1BU; tel. 0171 388 9888. For information about voluntary work in local areas and across Europe

Volunteer Development Agency (N. Ireland); tel. 01232 236100

Working abroad

EURES (European Employment Services); contact via local Jobcentres or tel. 0114 259 6051. The Employment Service's arm which handles job vacancies across Europe

Overseas Placing Unit; contact via local Jobcentres or tel. 0114 259 6051. The Employment Service's arm which handles worldwide vacancies